William Shakespeare's Macbeth

A Critical Study

Govind Digambar Kokane

Published by

ATLANTIC

PUBLISHERS & DISTRIBUTORS (P) LTD

7/22, Ansari Road, Darya Ganj, New Delhi-110002
Phones : +91-11-40775252, 40775214, 23273880, 23275880
Fax : +91-11-23285873
Web : www.atlanticbooks.com
E-mail : orders@atlanticbooks.com

Branch Office: Chennai
Phones : +91-44-48531784, 28291383
E-mail : chennai@atlanticbooks.com

Printed & bound in India by Atlantic Print Services

The book has been Dedicated to

My Philosophical Mother
Sharada Digambar Kokane

and

Social Activist Father
Digambar Lakshman Kokane

Preface

Macbeth, in five acts, is a tragedy by William Shakespeare. It is thought to have been first performed in 1606 and was printed for the first time in the folio of 1623, where it comes between *Julius Caesar* and *Hamlet*, and occupies pages 131–151. It is divided throughout into acts and scenes. It is the shortest of Shakespeare's tragedies, without diversions or sub-plots. It dramatises the damaging physical and psychological effects of political ambition on those who seek power for its own sake. The play follows the character of Macbeth, a bold Scottish general, as he becomes power-hungry and demented with political ambition. Shakespeare brilliantly portrays Macbeth and Lady Macbeth's downward spiral as they struggle with the punishing physical and psychological effects of greed.

The present book aims at a detailed study of *Macbeth*, dealing with the theme of ambition and fear. It organizes its material in terms of characterization, themes, and structure. It starts with an introductory chapter discussing Shakespeare's life, his works, and his times. Since the play is set primarily in Scotland, a brief history of Scotland has also been provided along with an outline of the play. The complete text of the play has been provided in the second chapter, and its summary with critical analysis in the third chapter of the book. The next three chapters deal with characterization, themes, and structure of the play. The last chapter concludes the study of the play and recommends further readings.

The book provides a detailed analysis on acts and scenes. It also examines the techniques and literary devices used, and provides selected reading materials which would provide the students with enough inspiration to pursue their study of drama independently.

William Shakespeare is a world famous dramatist. He has presented various aspects of human life through his plays. He was a great observer of human life. Human life is a mystery. The keen studies of great plays help us to understand life with all its intricacies. With the study of great plays, we develop our own view of life; we realize the true path of human life. His plays provide us immense knowledge of human life which is true for all times and all nations. His plays deal with themes of eternal importance. Passions and thoughts play an important role in human life. We should control the evil desires and live our life in the direction of sacred thoughts and emotions. Evil passions and thoughts create much chaos and confusion in our lives. We should be master of our emotions and not the slaves.

According to Aristotle, a play should bring about the purification of the emotions of the spectators. The studied play does it marvelously. It arouses the feelings of pity and fear among the audience; they feel pity for the tragic hero and the fear for themselves—the fear of occurring the same type of incident in their own lives. The play offers us great understanding of the human life.

Dr. Govind Digambar Kokane

Acknowledgements

I take this opportunity to express a deep sense of gratitude towards Dr. Anar Salunke, Director, Dr. Babasaheb Ambedkar Marathwada University, Sub-campus, Osmanabad, for her encouragement and guidance. I am thankful to Dr. Ramesh Chougule, Head, Department of English, Dr. Babasaheb Ambedkar Marathwada University, Sub-campus, Osmanabad, for his moral support and cooperation. I express thanks to all my friends and colleagues in the Department, Prof. H.P. Garad, Prof. P.B. Bansode, Dr. R.K. Mali, and Prof. V.G. Bhoval, who have always been kind and generous to me. I would like to express thanks to Dr. Anand Ubale, Associate Professor, Department of English, Dr. Babasaheb Ambedkar Marathwada University, Aurangabad, for his valuable suggestions and support. I express my gratitude towards my brothers Nagnath, Balaji, Aakash, and sisters Chitra and Hema for their valuable suggestions and guidance.

I express thanks to my wife Ira, daughter Anushka, and son Omkar, who have always been supportive and cooperative in my each endeavours. Their consistent cooperation inspires me a lot.

Dr. Govind Digambar Kokane

Contents

1
Introduction

1.0 Objectives

After studying this unit you will be able:

- to know about William Shakespeare's life and works
- to understand the culture of Shakespeare's time
- to get acquainted with Scottish History
- to have knowledge about the play *Macbeth* and its sources.

1.1 Introduction

In this unit, we learn about Shakespeare's life and works. His poetic and dramatic career has been divided into four periods. We also study the climate of ideas in his times and have information about the History of Scotland, Holinshed's *Chronicle* and Scott's *The Discoverie of Witchcraft* as a background to study the particular treatment Shakespeare has given to the play, *Macbeth*. *Macbeth* is a blend of fact, fable, and fancy.

1.2 Shakespeare's Life

Life of William Shakespeare: He had three children, namely Susanna, Hamnet, and Judith. Hamnet died at the young age of eleven. By that time, Shakespeare was already a successful playwright. He died on April 23, 1616.

1.3 Shakespeare's Works

William Shakespeare's poetic and dramatic career has been divided into four periods. The division corresponds to the growth and experience of his life and mind. These divisions are as follows:

(a) **Period of Early Experimentation (1588-93):** *Titus Andronicus*, *Henry VI* (three parts), *Love's Labour's*

Lost, *Comedy of Errors*, *Two Gentlemen of Verona*, *Richard III*, *Richard II*, *Romeo and Juliet* belong to this period. He wrote two poems during this period: *Venus and Adonis* and *The Rape of Lucrece*. The work of this period is, as a whole, extremely slight in texture, the treatment of life is superficial, and there is no depth of thought and characterization. The art is evidently immature. The work is characterized by youthful liveliness of imagination, by extravagance of language, and by a constant use of puns, conceits and other affectations.

(b) **Period of the Great Comedies and Chronicle Plays (1594-1600):** The works of this period comprise *King John*, *The Merchant of Venice*, *Henry IV* (Part I and Part II), *Henry V*, *The Taming of the Shrew*, *The Merry Wives of Windsor*, *Much Ado About Nothing*, *As You Like It*, and *Twelfth Night*. These plays show a rapid growth and development in the poet's genius. They reflect a deeper knowledge of human life and human nature. The characterization and the humour have become more perceptive, thought has become more valuable, rime has largely been abandoned for prose and blank verse. The blank verse itself lost its inflexibility.

(c) **Period of the Great Tragedies and of Bitter Comedies (1601-07):** *Julius Caesar*, *Hamlet*, *All's Well That Ends Well*, *Measure for Measure*, *Troilus and Cressida*, *Othello*, *King Lear*, *Macbeth*, *Antony and Cleopatra*, *Coriolanus*, and *Timon of Athens* belong to this period. This is a period of gloom and depression and it marks the complete maturity of his powers. His dramatic power, his intellectual power, and his power of expression are at their highest. This is the time of his supreme masterpieces. His attention is, however, occupied exclusively with the darker side of human experience. The sins and weaknesses of man form the theme of his plays, the emphasis is thrown on evil, and the tone is either serious or ferocious.

(d) **Period of the Later Comedies or Dramatic Romances (1608-12):** The plays of this period are *Pericles*, *Cymbeline*, *The Winter's Tale*, *The Tempest*, and the unfinished *Henry VIII*. During this period, the temper of Shakespeare has changed from bitter and gloomy to serene and peaceful. The heavy clouds have melted away from the sky. A tender and gracious tone prevails. The groundwork is still furnished by tragic passion, but the evil is no longer permitted to have its way. The evil is controlled and conquered by the good. The plays of this period take us back to the joys of the simple life of nature. The new notes are the notes of mercy and forgiveness, reunion, and reconciliation.

(e) **Classification of Shakespeare's Plays in the Folio of 1623:**

Histories: *Henry VI, Richard III, Richard II, King John, Henry IV, Henry V, Henry VIII.*

Tragedies: *Titus Andronicus, Romeo and Juliet, Julius Caesar, Hamlet, Othello, King Lear, Macbeth, Antony and Cleopatra, Coriolanus, Cymbeline, Timon of Athens.*

Comedies: *Love's Labour's Lost, Comedy of Errors, Two Gentlemen of Verona, Midsummer Night's Dream, Merchant of Venice, Taming of the Shrew, Merry Wives of Windsor, Much Ado About Nothing, As You Like It, Twelfth Night, All's Well That Ends Well, Measure for Measure, Troilus and Cressida, The Winter's Tale*, and *The Tempest.*

1.4 Shakespeare and His Times

William Shakespeare wrote poems and plays during the age of Elizabethan period. He was influenced by the Renaissance intellectual conventions. While his dramas assert the hierarchy of order, they also reflect the reality of disorder. For Shakespeare and his audience, the prevailing intellectual mode was analogical. Analogical world view was inherited from the middle ages. The universal chain of being included God and angels, the man and woman, the animals, the vegetation, the stones, etc. Creation was graded in the unified manner. Man possessed both body and soul; he occupied a pivotal place in the great chain of being.

Analogical thinking also suggested hierarchy and order in the political monarchy. God was considered the ruler of the macrocosmic world. King was accepted as the ruler of the political realm. The body obeyed the soul. The world obeyed the creator, and subjects were obedient to the king. Shakespeare's audience believed in the influence of stars on human life. Romeo and Juliet have been described as star-crossed lovers.

Machiavelli, the Italian political thinker, made a significant influence on the people in Shakespeare's England. He made a distinction between politics and ethics. Worldly politics was not shaped by the desire of the God, but by the will, aspiration, shrewdness, virtue, and liveliness of man.

Elizabethan theatre was a primeval concern. It was made of wooden structure. People took keen interest in the drama. In 1633, there were nineteen permanent theatres in London for a town of 3,00,000 inhabitants. A trumpet blast started the performance. No women ever appeared on the stage and very few women went to see the performances on the stage. The Queen summoned the players to the court on special occasions.

1.5 Brief History of Scotland

Plays are embodiments of real life. William Shakespeare borrowed incidents and events from history to compose plot for his plays. To understand the play, we should be familiar with incidents in history. Duncan was the son of Finlay the Mormaer—the Sub-King or Ross, by Doada, daughter of Malcolm II. Finlay was killed in 1020, in an encounter with Malcolm II. It gave rise to a blood feud between Macbeth and Duncan, the successor of Malcolm II. He married Gruoch, the widow of Gilcomgin, the Mormaer of Moray, and during the infancy of his stepson, Lulach, became the Mormaer of Moray. When Thorfinn, the Earl of Caithness, was in arms against Duncan, Macbeth, then the commander of Duncan's forces went over to the enemy and treacherously murdered Duncan at Bothgowanan near Elgin in 1040. He then divided the kingdom with Thorfinn. He took for himself, the districts south and west of the Tay and the central district in which Scone was situated. He crushed an insurrection by Crinan, the father of Duncan, and ruled justly and ably for

17 years. His benefactions to the Church were remarkable. He represented the Celtic and northern element of the population. Duncan and his family represented Saxon manners.

In 1054, Siward, the Earl of Northambria, with the consent of Edward the Confessor, attacked Scotland and defeated Macbeth on July 27. Macbeth retired to North. Siward was able to establish Malcolm III as a King of Cumbria. Siward and Macbeth's powerful ally Thorfinn died in 1057. Malcolm attacked Macbeth and killed him at Laum-phanon on August 15. Lady Macbeth was the daughter of Boete, the son of Kenneth III, who was deposed and slain by Malcolm II. According to the rule of transitory, the succession ought to have reverted to her father's family after death of Malcolm, but the later murdered her only brother; he had probably murdered her father previously to place Duncan on throne. Her first husband was Gilcomgain, Mormaer of Moray, a powerful prince. Malcolm II surprised him in his castle and murdered him with 50 followers. Lady Macbeth escaped with her infant Lulach to Ross, and subsequently married Macbeth, the Mormaer of the province. Like Macbeth, she had blood to avenge the successor of Malcolm II.

Duncan I was son of Crinan, the lay Abbot of Dunkeld by Beatrice, a daughter of Malcolm II. In 1034, he succeeded his maternal grandfather on the throne, thus violating the principle of alternate succession from the two branches of the family. He attacked Northumbria but was defeated. He then went to north and tried to dispose his cousin, Thorfinn, Earl of Cess, but was defeated both on land and sea. His General went over to Thorfinn's side and slew him treacherously. He married a daughter of Siward, Earl of Northumbria. Malcolm III was the eldest son of Duncan I. After father's murder, he first took refuge with his grandfather, and then went over to England. Siward was sent to attack Scotland. Macbeth was defeated near Dunsinane in 1054. Malcolm attacked Macbeth in 1057. A few months later, revolt by the stepson of Macbeth was crushed. He first married Ingibrorg, the widow of Thorfinn, and Margaret, a sister of Atheling. He is described as a bold and fearless warrior. He was kind, generous, and frank in disposition.

Banquo and Fleance are not known to history. Macduff and Lady Macduff are not mentioned in historical records. Norway did not invade Scotland during Duncan's reign. Lady Macbeth's suicide is not mentioned in historical books.

William Shakespeare did not invent plots for his plays. He borrowed plots from various sources. In *Macbeth*, for depiction of witches, he took hints from Reginald Scot's *The Discoverie of Witchcraft*, and *Essay on Demonology*. Holinshed's *Chronicles of England, Scotland, and Ireland* is his chief source. Though *Macbeth* is based on a historical account, it is not a history play. It is one of the maturest tragedies of the world. Shakespeare has shown originality in the creation of supernatural atmosphere in the play. The play *Macbeth* has been set in medieval Scotland. It is partly based on a true historical account. It is about the bloody rise to power and tragic downfall of the warrior, Macbeth.

Macbeth was a real king of Scotland in eleventh century. Shakespeare had read the story in Holinshed's *Chronicles*. He used the historical events described in the book for composition of many historical plays.

1.6 Outline of the Play

Macbeth is the shortest of William Shakespeare's great tragedies. It is without the complications of a subplot like a very few other Shakespearean plays. Therefore, action of the play moves forward fast. *Macbeth* has been set in Medieval Scotland. It is partly based on true historical account. It is the story about the bloody rise to power and tragic downfall of the warrior, Macbeth. The play deals with the theme of over ambition and its impact on life. Macbeth is already a successful general in the army of King Duncan. King Duncan of Scotland has been kind and considerate to his subjects. He has earned wide popularity and acclaim. Now he has grown old. Two of his nobles have revolted against him. These two nobles are the Thane of Cawdor and Macdonwald. In their revolt, they are aided and supported by the King of Norway. However, Macbeth, a distinguished general and close relative of King Duncan, and Banquo another general renowned for his courage and loyalty, fought so bravely that the rebels were soon routed, leaving thousands dead on the battlefield.

As soon as the battle is over, Macbeth and Banquo go the palace to inform King Duncan about their victory in the battle, and to get more instructions. They have to cross a heath on the way, where three witches greet them. They greet the two and welcome Macbeth as the Thane of Cawdor and foretell that he would soon be greater; he will be the King of Scotland. King Duncan becomes highly pleased when he gets the information about heroism of Macbeth and Banquo. He immediately orders the beheading of the defeated Thane of Cawdor. He sends noblemen of Scotland, Ross, and Angus, to welcome Macbeth with the title Thane of Cawdor. He was already Thane of Glamis.

Three witches tell a prophecy to Macbeth that he will be the King of Scotland in future. The witches also predict that future Scottish kings will descend from his fellow General Banquo, and not from Macbeth. Initially, Macbeth is prepared to wait for fate to take its course. When King Duncan nominates Malcolm as the next heir, Macbeth is stung by ambition and confusion. Lady Macbeth prodded him to murder King Duncan. Macbeth was ambitious. He already discussed with his wife about his dream to be the king. He writes to Lady Macbeth about the prophecy made by three witches.

King Duncan is deeply appreciative of the services of Macbeth and Banquo, as any right thinking monarch should be. He is simple-minded and trustful. He is full of gratitude towards those who have served him well. He would like to visit Macbeth's castle at Inverness in order to show his appreciation of Macbeth's great deeds on the battlefield.

Lady Macbeth reads a letter written to her by her husband after his meeting with the witches. After reading the letter, she believes that the crown is waiting for her husband. She also knows the obstacle in the way of attaining the throne. She knows that her husband is "too full of the milk of human kindness." A messenger comes to inform Lady Macbeth that the King of Scotland is coming to her castle that very night as a guest. Lady Macbeth considers this visit as a good opportunity for her husband to kill King Duncan. She is a woman of an iron determination and ruthless heart. In the beginning, Macbeth feels afraid of the consequences of the assassination of the king.

Lady Macbeth instigates her husband to kill the present king. Macbeth murders the king that very night. Macbeth also kills the two attendants as if in anger. Malcolm and Donalbain very cautiously run away. They are blamed for the murder. They must have bribed the two attendants. However, all this sounds so unnatural. There are people who are not convinced. They look at the whole affair with doubts and suspicion. The climax of the play is the assassination of Duncan.

Macbeth becomes the King of Scotland. Lady Macbeth is now the queen. The King and the Queen hold a royal feast at night. They invite most of the noblemen including Banquo. Macbeth requests Banquo to attend the banquet. Banquo promises to act in accordance with the King's command. Macbeth knows the superior virtues of Banquo's character. He possesses such royal dignity as would inspire awe in anyone. The prophecy of the witches troubles him. Witches predicted that throne will pass not to his own descendents but to Banquo's. Macbeth therefore thinks of killing Banquo and his son. Macbeth is not now the same simple-minded person whom we met early in the play. He has now become a seasoned intriguer. He urged two murderers to kill both Banquo and son, Fleance. From Banquo he diplomatically obtains the information regarding his movements during the day. He passes the information of Banquo's movements to the murderers. The murderers kill Banquo, but Fleance escapes. During the feast, Macbeth has hallucinations. He sees the ghost of Banquo seated in the empty chair meant for himself. Lady Macbeth saves the situation by her tact and self-control. Lenox, the Scottish nobleman, comments adversely on the actions of Macbeth. He indirectly accuses of having fixed the murders of Duncan and Banquo. Lenox says that the two sons of Duncan would also have been in great danger, if they had not fled from Scotland. Macbeth decides to meet the witches again to know more about his future from them. He asks them some questions regarding his future. They answer his questions with a show of apparitions. The first apparition is an armed head which tells Macbeth that he should be cautious of Macduff. The second apparition is a bloody child which tells Macbeth that he can defy the power of man because none of woman born shall ever be able to harm him. The third apparition is a crowned child holding a tree in its hand. From this apparition, Macbeth learns that he will never be defeated in the battle till Birnam Wood moves to Dunsinane hill. The witches show him eight kings followed by Banquo who holds a mirror in his hand and smiling at Macbeth. It becomes clear to Macbeth that the eight kings symbolize Banquo's descendents who are to sway over Scotland.

Macbeth decides to follow the advice given by the witches. He becomes bloody and bold. He is now completely dominated by the lust for power and has discarded his moral conscience. He orders the ruffians to murder the innocent Lady Macduff and her son. Macbeth has now become a hardened tyrant. Macduff had not come at his invitation to Scone. Macduff behaves like a most irresponsible husband. He has not done anything for the security of his family. He lacks sense of duty towards his wife and children. Not all his patriotism and integrity can remove the feeling of his lack of duty towards his family. Macduff's wife and children are brutally murdered. Macduff runs away to England to join Malcolm who is already there. The friendly king of England has already promised Malcolm to help with ten thousand soldiers. Soon they come to rescue their homeland from tyranny of Macbeth. Large numbers of Macbeth's subjects, who cannot endure his tyranny, join them.

Lady Macbeth feels mentally disturbed. She walks in her sleep during the night. She talks to herself in the course of her sleep-walking, all her talk is about the murder of King Duncan, the murder of Banquo, and the murder of Lady Macduff. The murder weighs heavily upon her mind. She has lost the peace of mind. She dies soon when her husband requires her help and support most. Macbeth retains some measure of self-control, till he gets the information that Birnam Wood was moving towards Dunsinane. In reality, the marching English armies had cut down the branches of trees, and were using them to cover their numbers.

Macbeth is entirely demoralized by the news of English army approaching towards Dunsinane. Macbeth thinks that the situation is almost hopeless. He has some hopes left. He believes the prophecy made by witches that he cannot be killed by any man born of woman. A fierce war was fought for a long time.

There is death and destruction all around. Macbeth fights most fiercely till he comes across Macduff. Macduff tells him that he was the man not born of woman; he was taken out of his mother's womb through ceaseration operation. Macbeth now realizes that the witches are equivocating fiends. Their lies are seeming truths. They deceive by a show of truth.

Macduff kills Macbeth and carries his head to Malcolm who is now unanimously elected as the future king of Scotland. He invites all those present for his coronation at Sconce, and promises to reward them all suitably for their services. Macbeth represents disorder and tyranny in the realm. Order would once again be established by the legitimate king of the country, Malcolm.

1.7 *Macbeth* and its Sources

William Shakespeare did not invent plot for his plays. He borrowed them from different sources. His plays are valuable criticism of human life. Probably *Macbeth* was written in 1606. He got the story for his play from Holinshed's *Chronicles of England, Scotland, and Ireland*. Holinshed's work was a historical compilation which provided Shakespeare with much of the material for the ten plays that were grouped under the title "Histories." Macbeth is not a history play. Macbeth was entitled a tragedy. Shakespeare deviated from his source in several respects for his dramatic purpose.

He used the scenes from Reginald Scot's *The Discoverie of Witchcraft* and *Essay on Demonology*. Shakespeare has shown his originality in the creation of supernatural atmosphere in the play. Macbeth is one of the maturest tragedies of the world. In Holinshed's *Chronicles*, King Duncan is killed in a battle with Macbeth, while in Shakespeare's play, he is murdered in sleep. Shakespeare has deviated from the source according to the dramatic necessity.

Macbeth was a real king of Scotland in eleventh-century Scotland. Shakespeare had read the history from several sources. In Holinshed's account, Macbeth and Banquo combine to kill King Duncan. The original story is full of wonderful details that show the cunning of the Scots. Macbeth slaughtered an entire Danish army not by brute force, but cunning. He mixed a sleeping potion, and sent it as a gift to the enemy army. Once they were asleep, Macbeth killed them easily. In Holinshed's account, Macbeth's wife is ambitious to become the queen, but Lady Macbeth does not feature as a partner in crime. Instead Banquo join forces with Macbeth to kill King Duncan. Holinshed provided Shakespeare with a good story. *Macbeth* contains many examples of imagery and language Shakespeare directly borrowed from the source. It was a practice common to all writers.

1.8 Check your Progress

(1) Write a short note on William Shakespeare's life and works.

(2) How did Shakespeare's time influence his creative writing?

(3) How does the play *Macbeth* refer to Scottish history?

(4) What is the outline story of the play, *Macbeth*?

(5) What sources did William Shakespeare use in the composition of *Macbeth*?

1.9 Key to Check your Progress

(1) For answer see 1.2 and 1.3

(2) For answer see 1.4

(3) For answer see 1.5

(4) For answer see 1.6

(5) For answer see 1.7

1.10 Summary

We have learnt that William Shakespeare's thirty-seven plays are often divided into four periods corresponding to the growth and experience of his life and mind. Briefly, we have studied the important ideas and thoughts of his audience. We have also studied the Scottish History and Holinshed's *Chronicles* to understand the particular treatment Shakespeare has given to *Macbeth*. Now we know that Shakespeare borrowed material from various sources for *Macbeth*. It would be interesting to study the difference and resemblances between Shakespeare and Holinshed's Macbeth.

1.11 Glossary

- Ambition—a strong desire to achieve something
- Cunning—clever at deceiving people
- Prod—to make or try to make a slow or unwilling person to do something
- Prophecy—a statement that tells what will happen in the future
- Heath—an area of open wild land covered with rough grass and low plants; a small area of moorland
- Tragedy—a serious play with a sad ending
- Comedy—a light or amusing play usually with a happy ending
- Plot—a plan or outline of the events in a play
- Succession—the action, process or right of succeeding to a title, property, etc.

1.12 Further Reading

Biggins, D. "Sexuality, Witchcraft and Violence in Macbeth." *Shakespeare Studies.*

Booth, Stephen. "*Macbeth,* Aristotle, Definition, and Tragedy." *King Lear, Macbeth, in Definition, and Tragedy*. New Haven: Yale University Press, 1983, 79-118.

Knights, L.C. "How Many Children had Lady Macbeth? An Essay in the Theory and Practice of Shakespeare Criticism." *Explorations*. New York University Press, 1964, 15-54.

Williams, Raymond. "Monologue in *Macbeth.*" *Teaching the Text*. Ed. Susanne Kappeler and Norman Bryson. London: Routledge & Kegan Paul, 1983, 180-202, 282-99.

1.13 Recommended Reading

Bradley, A.C. *Shakespearean Tragedy: Lectures on Hamlet, Othello, King Lear, Macbeth.* New York: Penguin, 1991.

Coleridge, Samuel, Foakes, R.A. and Collier, John. eds. *Coleridge on Shakespeare: The Text of the Lectures of 1811-12.* London: Routledge, 2005.

Harley, Granville-Barker. *Prefaces to Shakespeare*. New Delhi: Atlantic Publishers & Distributors, 2007.

Harold, Bloom. *Shakespeare: The Invention of the Human*. New York: Riverhead Books, 1998.

Hudson, William. *An Introduction to the Study of Literature*. New Delhi: Rupa Publications, 2015.

2
The Complete Text of the Play

Macbeth

WILLIAM SHAKESPEARE

DRAMATIS PERSONAE

DUNCAN, King of Scotland

MACBETH, Thane of Glamis and Cawdor, a general in the King's army

LADY MACBETH, his wife

MACDUFF, Thane of Fife, a nobleman of Scotland

LADY MACDUFF, his wife

MALCOLM, elder son of Duncan

DONALBAIN, younger son of Duncan

BANQUO, a general in the King's army

FLEANCE, his son

LENNOX, nobleman of Scotland

ROSS, nobleman of Scotland

MENTEITH nobleman of Scotland

ANGUS, nobleman of Scotland

CAITHNESS, nobleman of Scotland

SIWARD, Earl of Northumberland, general of the English forces

YOUNG SIWARD, his son

SEYTON, attendant to Macbeth

HECATE, Queen of the Witches

The Three Witches

Boy, Son of Macduff

Gentlewoman attending on Lady Macbeth

An English Doctor

A Scottish Doctor

A Sergeant

A Porter

An Old Man

The Ghost of Banquo and other Apparitions

Lords, Gentlemen, Officers, Soldiers, Murderers, Attendants, and Messengers

The Tragedy of Macbeth

William Shakespeare

ACT I

SCENE I. A desert Place

Thunder and lightning. Enter three Witches

First Witch

When shall we three meet again
In thunder, lightning, or in rain?

Second Witch

When the hurlyburly's done,
When the battle's lost and won.

Third Witch

That will be ere the set of sun.

First Witch

Where the place?

Second Witch

Upon the heath.

Third Witch

There to meet with Macbeth.

First Witch

I come, Graymalkin!

Second Witch

Paddock calls.

Third Witch

Anon.

ALL

Fair is foul, and foul is fair:
Hover through the fog and filthy air.

Exeunt

SCENE II. A camp near Forres

Alarum within. Enter DUNCAN, MALCOLM, DONALBAIN, LENNOX, with Attendants, meeting a bleeding Sergeant

DUNCAN

What bloody man is that? He can report,
As seemeth by his plight, of the revolt
The newest state.

MALCOLM

This is the sergeant
Who like a good and hardy soldier fought
'Gainst my captivity. Hail, brave friend!
Say to the king the knowledge of the broil
As thou didst leave it.

Sergeant

Doubtful it stood;
As two spent swimmers, that do cling together
And choke their art. The merciless Macdonwald—
Worthy to be a rebel, for to that
The multiplying villanies of nature
Do swarm upon him—from the western isles
Of kerns and gallowglasses is supplied;
And fortune, on his damned quarrel smiling,

Show'd like a rebel's whore: but all's too weak:
For brave Macbeth—well he deserves that name—
Disdaining fortune, with his brandish'd steel,
Which smoked with bloody execution,
Like valour's minion carved out his passage
Till he faced the slave;
Which ne'er shook hands, nor bade farewell to him,
Till he unseam'd him from the nave to the chops,
And fix'd his head upon our battlements.

DUNCAN

O valiant cousin! worthy gentleman!

Sergeant

As whence the sun 'gins his reflection
Shipwrecking storms and direful thunders break,
So from that spring whence comfort seem'd to come
Discomfort swells. Mark, king of Scotland, mark:
No sooner justice had with valour arm'd
Compell'd these skipping kerns to trust their heels,
But the Norweyan lord surveying vantage,
With furbish'd arms and new supplies of men
Began a fresh assault.

DUNCAN

Dismay'd not this
Our captains, Macbeth and Banquo?

Sergeant

Yes;
As sparrows eagles, or the hare the lion.
If I say sooth, I must report they were
As cannons overcharged with double cracks, so they
Doubly redoubled strokes upon the foe:
Except they meant to bathe in reeking wounds,
Or memorise another Golgotha,
I cannot tell.
But I am faint, my gashes cry for help.

DUNCAN

So well thy words become thee as thy wounds;
They smack of honour both. Go get him surgeons.

Exit Sergeant, attended

Who comes here?

Enter ROSS

MALCOLM

The worthy thane of Ross.

LENNOX

What a haste looks through his eyes! So should he look
That seems to speak things strange.

ROSS

God save the king!

DUNCAN

Whence camest thou, worthy thane?

ROSS

From Fife, great king;
Where the Norweyan banners flout the sky
And fan our people cold. Norway himself,
With terrible numbers,
Assisted by that most disloyal traitor
The thane of Cawdor, began a dismal conflict;
Till that Bellona's bridegroom, lapp'd in proof,
Confronted him with self-comparisons,
Point against point rebellious, arm 'gainst arm.
Curbing his lavish spirit: and, to conclude,
The victory fell on us.

DUNCAN

Great happiness!

ROSS

That now
Sweno, the Norways' king, craves composition:
Nor would we deign him burial of his men

Till he disbursed at Saint Colme's inch
Ten thousand dollars to our general use.

DUNCAN

No more that thane of Cawdor shall deceive
Our bosom interest: go pronounce his present death,
And with his former title greet Macbeth.

ROSS

I'll see it done.

DUNCAN

What he hath lost noble Macbeth hath won.

Exeunt

SCENE III. A heath near Forres

Thunder. Enter the three Witches

First Witch

Where hast thou been, sister?

Second Witch

Killing swine.

Third Witch

Sister, where thou?

First Witch

A sailor's wife had chestnuts in her lap,
And munch'd, and munch'd, and munch'd:—
'Give me,' quoth I:
'Aroint thee, witch!' the rump-fed ronyon cries.
Her husband's to Aleppo gone, master o' the Tiger:
But in a sieve I'll thither sail,
And, like a rat without a tail,
I'll do, I'll do, and I'll do.

Second Witch

I'll give thee a wind.

First Witch

Thou'rt kind.

Third Witch

And I another.

First Witch

I myself have all the other,
And the very ports they blow,
All the quarters that they know
I' the shipman's card.
I will drain him dry as hay:
Sleep shall neither night nor day
Hang upon his pent-house lid;
He shall live a man forbid:
Weary sev'nights nine times nine
Shall he dwindle, peak and pine:
Though his bark cannot be lost,
Yet it shall be tempest-tost.
Look what I have.

Second Witch

Show me, show me.

First Witch

Here I have a pilot's thumb,
Wreck'd as homeward he did come.

Drum within

Third Witch

A drum, a drum!
Macbeth doth come.

ALL

The weird sisters, hand in hand,
Posters of the sea and land,
Thus do go about, about:
Thrice to thine and thrice to mine
And thrice again, to make up nine.
Peace! the charm's wound up.

Enter MACBETH and BANQUO

MACBETH

So foul and fair a day I have not seen.

BANQUO

How far is't call'd to Forres? What are these
So wither'd and so wild in their attire,
That look not like the inhabitants o' the earth,
And yet are on't? Live you? or are you aught
That man may question? You seem to understand me,
By each at once her choppy finger laying
Upon her skinny lips: you should be women,
And yet your beards forbid me to interpret
That you are so.

MACBETH

Speak, if you can: what are you?

First Witch

All hail, Macbeth! hail to thee, thane of Glamis!

Second Witch

All hail, Macbeth, hail to thee, thane of Cawdor!

Third Witch

All hail, Macbeth, thou shalt be king hereafter!

BANQUO

Good sir, why do you start; and seem to fear
Things that do sound so fair? I' the name of truth,
Are ye fantastical, or that indeed
Which outwardly ye show? My noble partner
You greet with present grace and great prediction
Of noble having and of royal hope,
That he seems rapt withal: to me you speak not.
If you can look into the seeds of time,
And say which grain will grow and which will not,
Speak then to me, who neither beg nor fear
Your favours nor your hate.

First Witch

Hail!

Second Witch

Hail!

Third Witch

Hail!

First Witch

Lesser than Macbeth, and greater.

Second Witch

Not so happy, yet much happier.

Third Witch

Thou shalt get kings, though thou be none:
So all hail, Macbeth and Banquo!

First Witch

Banquo and Macbeth, all hail!

MACBETH

Stay, you imperfect speakers, tell me more:
By Sinel's death I know I am thane of Glamis;
But how of Cawdor? the thane of Cawdor lives,
A prosperous gentleman; and to be king
Stands not within the prospect of belief,
No more than to be Cawdor. Say from whence
You owe this strange intelligence? or why
Upon this blasted heath you stop our way
With such prophetic greeting? Speak, I charge you.
Witches vanish

BANQUO

The earth hath bubbles, as the water has,
And these are of them. Whither are they vanish'd?

MACBETH

Into the air; and what seem'd corporal melted
As breath into the wind. Would they had stay'd!

BANQUO

Were such things here as we do speak about?
Or have we eaten on the insane root
That takes the reason prisoner?

MACBETH

Your children shall be kings.

BANQUO

You shall be king.

MACBETH

And thane of Cawdor too: went it not so?

BANQUO

To the selfsame tune and words. Who's here?

Enter ROSS and ANGUS

ROSS

The king hath happily received, Macbeth,
The news of thy success; and when he reads
Thy personal venture in the rebels' fight,
His wonders and his praises do contend
Which should be thine or his: silenced with that,
In viewing o'er the rest o' the selfsame day,
He finds thee in the stout Norweyan ranks,
Nothing afeard of what thyself didst make,
Strange images of death. As thick as hail
Came post with post; and every one did bear
Thy praises in his kingdom's great defence,
And pour'd them down before him.

ANGUS

We are sent
To give thee from our royal master thanks;
Only to herald thee into his sight,
Not pay thee.

ROSS

And, for an earnest of a greater honour,
He bade me, from him, call thee thane of Cawdor:
In which addition, hail, most worthy thane!
For it is thine.

BANQUO

What, can the devil speak true?

MACBETH

The thane of Cawdor lives: why do you dress me
In borrow'd robes?

ANGUS

Who was the thane lives yet;
But under heavy judgment bears that life
Which he deserves to lose. Whether he was combined
With those of Norway, or did line the rebel
With hidden help and vantage, or that with both
He labour'd in his country's wreck, I know not;
But treasons capital, confess'd and proved,
Have overthrown him.

MACBETH

[Aside] Glamis, and thane of Cawdor!
The greatest is behind.

To ROSS and ANGUS

Thanks for your pains.

To BANQUO

Do you not hope your children shall be kings,
When those that gave the thane of Cawdor to me
Promised no less to them?

BANQUO

That trusted home
Might yet enkindle you unto the crown,
Besides the thane of Cawdor. But 'tis strange:
And oftentimes, to win us to our harm,
The instruments of darkness tell us truths,
Win us with honest trifles, to betray's
In deepest consequence.
Cousins, a word, I pray you.

MACBETH

[Aside] Two truths are told,
As happy prologues to the swelling act
Of the imperial theme.—I thank you, gentlemen.

[Aside] This supernatural soliciting
Cannot be ill, cannot be good: if ill,
Why hath it given me earnest of success,
Commencing in a truth? I am thane of Cawdor:
If good, why do I yield to that suggestion
Whose horrid image doth unfix my hair
And make my seated heart knock at my ribs,
Against the use of nature? Present fears
Are less than horrible imaginings:
My thought, whose murder yet is but fantastical,
Shakes so my single state of man that function
Is smother'd in surmise, and nothing is
But what is not.

BANQUO

Look, how our partner's rapt.

MACBETH

[Aside] If chance will have me king, why, chance may crown me,
Without my stir.

BANQUO

New honours come upon him,
Like our strange garments, cleave not to their mould
But with the aid of use.

MACBETH

[Aside] Come what come may,
Time and the hour runs through the roughest day.

BANQUO

Worthy Macbeth, we stay upon your leisure.

MACBETH

Give me your favour: my dull brain was wrought
With things forgotten. Kind gentlemen, your pains
Are register'd where every day I turn
The leaf to read them. Let us toward the king.
Think upon what hath chanced, and, at more time,
The interim having weigh'd it, let us speak
Our free hearts each to other.

BANQUO

Very gladly.

MACBETH

Till then, enough. Come, friends.

Exeunt

SCENE IV. Forres. The palace

Flourish. Enter DUNCAN, MALCOLM, DONALBAIN, LENNOX, and Attendants

DUNCAN

Is execution done on Cawdor? Are not
Those in commission yet return'd?

MALCOLM

My liege,
They are not yet come back. But I have spoke
With one that saw him die: who did report
That very frankly he confess'd his treasons,
Implored your highness' pardon and set forth
A deep repentance: nothing in his life
Became him like the leaving it; he died
As one that had been studied in his death
To throw away the dearest thing he owed,
As 'twere a careless trifle.

DUNCAN

There's no art
To find the mind's construction in the face:
He was a gentleman on whom I built
An absolute trust.

Enter MACBETH, BANQUO, ROSS, and ANGUS

O worthiest cousin!
The sin of my ingratitude even now
Was heavy on me: thou art so far before
That swiftest wing of recompense is slow
To overtake thee. Would thou hadst less deserved,
That the proportion both of thanks and payment
Might have been mine! only I have left to say,
More is thy due than more than all can pay.

MACBETH

The service and the loyalty I owe,
In doing it, pays itself. Your highness' part
Is to receive our duties; and our duties
Are to your throne and state children and servants,
Which do but what they should, by doing every thing
Safe toward your love and honour.

DUNCAN

Welcome hither:
I have begun to plant thee, and will labour
To make thee full of growing. Noble Banquo,
That hast no less deserved, nor must be known
No less to have done so, let me enfold thee
And hold thee to my heart.

BANQUO

There if I grow,
The harvest is your own.

DUNCAN

My plenteous joys,
Wanton in fulness, seek to hide themselves
In drops of sorrow. Sons, kinsmen, thanes,
And you whose places are the nearest, know
We will establish our estate upon
Our eldest, Malcolm, whom we name hereafter
The Prince of Cumberland; which honour must
Not unaccompanied invest him only,
But signs of nobleness, like stars, shall shine
On all deservers. From hence to Inverness,
And bind us further to you.

MACBETH

The rest is labour, which is not used for you:
I'll be myself the harbinger and make joyful
The hearing of my wife with your approach;
So humbly take my leave.

DUNCAN

My worthy Cawdor!

MACBETH

[Aside] The Prince of Cumberland! that is a step
On which I must fall down, or else o'erleap,
For in my way it lies. Stars, hide your fires;
Let not light see my black and deep desires:
The eye wink at the hand; yet let that be,
Which the eye fears, when it is done, to see.

Exit

DUNCAN

True, worthy Banquo; he is full so valiant,
And in his commendations I am fed;
It is a banquet to me. Let's after him,
Whose care is gone before to bid us welcome:
It is a peerless kinsman.

Flourish. Exeunt

SCENE V. Inverness. Macbeth's castle

Enter LADY MACBETH, reading a letter

LADY MACBETH

'They met me in the day of success: and I have learned by the perfectest report, they have more in them than mortal knowledge. When I burned in desire to question them further, they made themselves air, into which they vanished. Whiles I stood rapt in the wonder of it, came missives from the king, who all-hailed me 'Thane of Cawdor;' by which title, before, these weird sisters saluted me, and referred me to the coming on of time, with 'Hail, king that shalt be!' This have I thought good to deliver thee, my dearest partner of greatness, that thou mightst not lose the dues of rejoicing, by being ignorant of what greatness is promised thee. Lay it to thy heart, and farewell.'

Glamis thou art, and Cawdor; and shalt be
What thou art promised: yet do I fear thy nature;
It is too full o' the milk of human kindness

To catch the nearest way: thou wouldst be great;
Art not without ambition, but without
The illness should attend it: what thou wouldst highly,
That wouldst thou holily; wouldst not play false,
And yet wouldst wrongly win: thou'ldst have, great Glamis,
That which cries "Thus thou must do, if thou have it;
And that which rather thou dost fear to do
Than wishest should be undone." Hie thee hither,
That I may pour my spirits in thine ear;
And chastise with the valour of my tongue
All that impedes thee from the golden round,
Which fate and metaphysical aid doth seem
To have thee crown'd withal.
Enter a Messenger
What is your tidings?

Messenger

The king comes here to-night.

LADY MACBETH

Thou'rt mad to say it:
Is not thy master with him? who, were't so,
Would have inform'd for preparation.

Messenger

So please you, it is true: our thane is coming:
One of my fellows had the speed of him,
Who, almost dead for breath, had scarcely more
Than would make up his message.

LADY MACBETH

Give him tending;
He brings great news.

Exit Messenger

The raven himself is hoarse
That croaks the fatal entrance of Duncan
Under my battlements. Come, you spirits
That tend on mortal thoughts, unsex me here,
And fill me from the crown to the toe top-full
Of direst cruelty! make thick my blood;

Stop up the access and passage to remorse,
That no compunctious visitings of nature
Shake my fell purpose, nor keep peace between
The effect and it! Come to my woman's breasts,
And take my milk for gall, you murdering ministers,
Wherever in your sightless substances
You wait on nature's mischief! Come, thick night,
And pall thee in the dunnest smoke of hell,
That my keen knife see not the wound it makes,
Nor heaven peep through the blanket of the dark,
To cry 'Hold, hold!'

Enter MACBETH

Great Glamis! worthy Cawdor!
Greater than both, by the all-hail hereafter!
Thy letters have transported me beyond
This ignorant present, and I feel now
The future in the instant.

MACBETH

My dearest love,
Duncan comes here to-night.

LADY MACBETH

And when goes hence?

MACBETH

To-morrow, as he purposes.

LADY MACBETH

O, never
Shall sun that morrow see!
Your face, my thane, is as a book where men
May read strange matters. To beguile the time,
Look like the time; bear welcome in your eye,
Your hand, your tongue: look like the innocent flower,
But be the serpent under't. He that's coming
Must be provided for: and you shall put
This night's great business into my dispatch;
Which shall to all our nights and days to come
Give solely sovereign sway and masterdom.

MACBETH

We will speak further.

LADY MACBETH

Only look up clear;
To alter favour ever is to fear:
Leave all the rest to me.

Exeunt

SCENE VI. Before Macbeth's castle

Hautboys and torches. Enter DUNCAN, MALCOLM, DONALBAIN, BANQUO, LENNOX, MACDUFF, ROSS, ANGUS, and Attendants

DUNCAN

This castle hath a pleasant seat; the air
Nimbly and sweetly recommends itself
Unto our gentle senses.

BANQUO

This guest of summer,
The temple-haunting martlet, does approve,
By his loved mansionry, that the heaven's breath
Smells wooingly here: no jutty, frieze,
Buttress, nor coign of vantage, but this bird
Hath made his pendent bed and procreant cradle:
Where they most breed and haunt, I have observed,
The air is delicate.

Enter LADY MACBETH

DUNCAN

See, see, our honour'd hostess!
The love that follows us sometime is our trouble,
Which still we thank as love. Herein I teach you
How you shall bid God 'ild us for your pains,
And thank us for your trouble.

LADY MACBETH

All our service
In every point twice done and then done double
Were poor and single business to contend

Against those honours deep and broad wherewith
Your majesty loads our house: for those of old,
And the late dignities heap'd up to them,
We rest your hermits.

DUNCAN

Where's the thane of Cawdor?
We coursed him at the heels, and had a purpose
To be his purveyor: but he rides well;
And his great love, sharp as his spur, hath holp him
To his home before us. Fair and noble hostess,
We are your guest to-night.

LADY MACBETH

Your servants ever
Have theirs, themselves and what is theirs, in compt,
To make their audit at your highness' pleasure,
Still to return your own.

DUNCAN

Give me your hand;
Conduct me to mine host: we love him highly,
And shall continue our graces towards him.
By your leave, hostess.

Exeunt

SCENE VII. Macbeth's castle

Hautboys and torches. Enter a Sewer, and divers Servants with dishes and service, and pass over the stage. Then enter MACBETH

MACBETH

If it were done when 'tis done, then 'twere well
It were done quickly: if the assassination
Could trammel up the consequence, and catch
With his surcease success; that but this blow
Might be the be-all and the end-all here,
But here, upon this bank and shoal of time,
We'ld jump the life to come. But in these cases
We still have judgment here; that we but teach
Bloody instructions, which, being taught, return

To plague the inventor: this even-handed justice
Commends the ingredients of our poison'd chalice
To our own lips. He's here in double trust;
First, as I am his kinsman and his subject,
Strong both against the deed; then, as his host,
Who should against his murderer shut the door,
Not bear the knife myself. Besides, this Duncan
Hath borne his faculties so meek, hath been
So clear in his great office, that his virtues
Will plead like angels, trumpet-tongued, against
The deep damnation of his taking-off;
And pity, like a naked new-born babe,
Striding the blast, or heaven's cherubim, horsed
Upon the sightless couriers of the air,
Shall blow the horrid deed in every eye,
That tears shall drown the wind. I have no spur
To prick the sides of my intent, but only
Vaulting ambition, which o'erleaps itself
And falls on the other.

Enter LADY MACBETH

How now! what news?

LADY MACBETH

He has almost supp'd: why have you left the chamber?

MACBETH

Hath he ask'd for me?

LADY MACBETH

Know you not he has?

MACBETH

We will proceed no further in this business:
He hath honour'd me of late; and I have bought
Golden opinions from all sorts of people,
Which would be worn now in their newest gloss,
Not cast aside so soon.

LADY MACBETH

Was the hope drunk
Wherein you dress'd yourself? hath it slept since?

And wakes it now, to look so green and pale
At what it did so freely? From this time
Such I account thy love. Art thou afeard
To be the same in thine own act and valour
As thou art in desire? Wouldst thou have that
Which thou esteem'st the ornament of life,
And live a coward in thine own esteem,
Letting 'I dare not' wait upon 'I would,'
Like the poor cat i' the adage?

MACBETH

Prithee, peace:
I dare do all that may become a man;
Who dares do more is none.

LADY MACBETH

What beast was't, then,
That made you break this enterprise to me?
When you durst do it, then you were a man;
And, to be more than what you were, you would
Be so much more the man. Nor time nor place
Did then adhere, and yet you would make both:
They have made themselves, and that their fitness now
Does unmake you. I have given suck, and know
How tender 'tis to love the babe that milks me:
I would, while it was smiling in my face,
Have pluck'd my nipple from his boneless gums,
And dash'd the brains out, had I so sworn as you
Have done to this.

MACBETH

If we should fail?

LADY MACBETH

We fail!
But screw your courage to the sticking-place,
And we'll not fail. When Duncan is asleep—
Whereto the rather shall his day's hard journey
Soundly invite him—his two chamberlains
Will I with wine and wassail so convince
That memory, the warder of the brain,

Shall be a fume, and the receipt of reason
A limbeck only: when in swinish sleep
Their drenched natures lie as in a death,
What cannot you and I perform upon
The unguarded Duncan? what not put upon
His spongy officers, who shall bear the guilt
Of our great quell?

MACBETH

Bring forth men-children only;
For thy undaunted mettle should compose
Nothing but males. Will it not be received,
When we have mark'd with blood those sleepy two
Of his own chamber and used their very daggers,
That they have done't?

LADY MACBETH

Who dares receive it other,
As we shall make our griefs and clamour roar
Upon his death?

MACBETH

I am settled, and bend up
Each corporal agent to this terrible feat.
Away, and mock the time with fairest show:
False face must hide what the false heart doth know.

Exeunt

ACT II

SCENE I. Court of Macbeth's castle

Enter BANQUO, and FLEANCE bearing a torch before him

BANQUO

How goes the night, boy?

FLEANCE

The moon is down; I have not heard the clock.

BANQUO

And she goes down at twelve.

FLEANCE

I take't, 'tis later, sir.

BANQUO

Hold, take my sword. There's husbandry in heaven;
Their candles are all out. Take thee that too.
A heavy summons lies like lead upon me,
And yet I would not sleep: merciful powers,
Restrain in me the cursed thoughts that nature
Gives way to in repose!

Enter MACBETH, and a Servant with a torch

Give me my sword.
Who's there?

MACBETH

A friend.

BANQUO

What, sir, not yet at rest? The king's a-bed:
He hath been in unusual pleasure, and
Sent forth great largess to your offices.
This diamond he greets your wife withal,
By the name of most kind hostess; and shut up
In measureless content.

MACBETH

Being unprepared,
Our will became the servant to defect;
Which else should free have wrought.

BANQUO

All's well.
I dreamt last night of the three weird sisters:
To you they have show'd some truth.

MACBETH

I think not of them:
Yet, when we can entreat an hour to serve,
We would spend it in some words upon that business,
If you would grant the time.

BANQUO

At your kind'st leisure.

MACBETH

If you shall cleave to my consent, when 'tis,
It shall make honour for you.

BANQUO

So I lose none
In seeking to augment it, but still keep
My bosom franchised and allegiance clear,
I shall be counsell'd.

MACBETH

Good repose the while!

BANQUO

Thanks, sir: the like to you!

Exeunt BANQUO and FLEANCE

MACBETH

Go bid thy mistress, when my drink is ready,
She strike upon the bell. Get thee to bed.

Exit Servant

Is this a dagger which I see before me,
The handle toward my hand? Come, let me clutch thee.
I have thee not, and yet I see thee still.
Art thou not, fatal vision, sensible
To feeling as to sight? or art thou but
A dagger of the mind, a false creation,
Proceeding from the heat-oppressed brain?
I see thee yet, in form as palpable
As this which now I draw.
Thou marshall'st me the way that I was going;
And such an instrument I was to use.
Mine eyes are made the fools o' the other senses,
Or else worth all the rest; I see thee still,
And on thy blade and dudgeon gouts of blood,
Which was not so before. There's no such thing:
It is the bloody business which informs

Thus to mine eyes. Now o'er the one halfworld
Nature seems dead, and wicked dreams abuse
The curtain'd sleep; witchcraft celebrates
Pale Hecate's offerings, and wither'd murder,
Alarum'd by his sentinel, the wolf,
Whose howl's his watch, thus with his stealthy pace.
With Tarquin's ravishing strides, towards his design
Moves like a ghost. Thou sure and firm-set earth,
Hear not my steps, which way they walk, for fear
Thy very stones prate of my whereabout,
And take the present horror from the time,
Which now suits with it. Whiles I threat, he lives:
Words to the heat of deeds too cold breath gives.
A bell rings

I go, and it is done; the bell invites me.
Hear it not, Duncan; for it is a knell
That summons thee to heaven or to hell.

Exit

SCENE II. The same

Enter LADY MACBETH

LADY MACBETH

That which hath made them drunk hath made me bold;
What hath quench'd them hath given me fire.
Hark! Peace!
It was the owl that shriek'd, the fatal bellman,
Which gives the stern'st good-night. He is about it:
The doors are open; and the surfeited grooms
Do mock their charge with snores: I have drugg'd their possets,
That death and nature do contend about them,
Whether they live or die.

MACBETH

[Within] Who's there? what, ho!

LADY MACBETH

Alack, I am afraid they have awaked,
And 'tis not done. The attempt and not the deed

Confounds us. Hark! I laid their daggers ready;
He could not miss 'em. Had he not resembled
My father as he slept, I had done't.

Enter MACBETH

My husband!

MACBETH

I have done the deed. Didst thou not hear a noise?

LADY MACBETH

I heard the owl scream and the crickets cry.
Did not you speak?

MACBETH

When?

LADY MACBETH

Now.

MACBETH

As I descended?

LADY MACBETH

Ay.

MACBETH

Hark!
Who lies i' the second chamber?

LADY MACBETH

Donalbain.

MACBETH

This is a sorry sight.

Looking on his hands

LADY MACBETH

A foolish thought, to say a sorry sight.

MACBETH

There's one did laugh in's sleep, and one cried 'Murder!'
That they did wake each other: I stood and heard them:

But they did say their prayers, and address'd them
Again to sleep.

LADY MACBETH

There are two lodged together.

MACBETH

One cried 'God bless us!' and 'Amen' the other;
As they had seen me with these hangman's hands.
Listening their fear, I could not say 'Amen,'
When they did say 'God bless us!'

LADY MACBETH

Consider it not so deeply.

MACBETH

But wherefore could not I pronounce 'Amen'?
I had most need of blessing, and 'Amen'
Stuck in my throat.

LADY MACBETH

These deeds must not be thought
After these ways; so, it will make us mad.

MACBETH

Methought I heard a voice cry "Sleep no more!
Macbeth does murder sleep", the innocent sleep,
Sleep that knits up the ravell'd sleeve of care,
The death of each day's life, sore labour's bath,
Balm of hurt minds, great nature's second course,
Chief nourisher in life's feast,—

LADY MACBETH

What do you mean?

MACBETH

Still it cried 'Sleep no more!' to all the house:
"Glamis hath murder'd sleep, and therefore Cawdor
Shall sleep no more; Macbeth shall sleep no more."

LADY MACBETH

Who was it that thus cried? Why, worthy thane,
You do unbend your noble strength, to think
So brainsickly of things. Go get some water,

And wash this filthy witness from your hand.
Why did you bring these daggers from the place?
They must lie there: go carry them; and smear
The sleepy grooms with blood.

MACBETH

I'll go no more:
I am afraid to think what I have done;
Look on't again I dare not.

LADY MACBETH

Infirm of purpose!
Give me the daggers: the sleeping and the dead
Are but as pictures: 'tis the eye of childhood
That fears a painted devil. If he do bleed,
I'll gild the faces of the grooms withal;
For it must seem their guilt.

Exit. Knocking within

MACBETH

Whence is that knocking?
How is't with me, when every noise appals me?
What hands are here? ha! they pluck out mine eyes.
Will all great Neptune's ocean wash this blood
Clean from my hand? No, this my hand will rather
The multitudinous seas in incarnadine,
Making the green one red.

Re-enter LADY MACBETH

LADY MACBETH

My hands are of your colour; but I shame
To wear a heart so white.

Knocking within

I hear a knocking
At the south entry: retire we to our chamber;
A little water clears us of this deed:
How easy is it, then! Your constancy
Hath left you unattended.

Knocking within

Hark! more knocking.
Get on your nightgown, lest occasion call us,

And show us to be watchers. Be not lost
So poorly in your thoughts.

MACBETH

To know my deed, 'twere best not know myself.

Knocking within

Wake Duncan with thy knocking! I would thou couldst!

Exeunt

SCENE III. The same

Knocking within. Enter a Porter

Porter

Here's a knocking indeed! If a
man were porter of hell-gate, he should have
old turning the key.

Knocking within

Knock,
knock, knock! Who's there, i' the name of
Beelzebub? Here's a farmer, that hanged
himself on the expectation of plenty: come in
time; have napkins enow about you; here
you'll sweat for't.

Knocking within

Knock,
knock! Who's there, in the other devil's
name? Faith, here's an equivocator, that could
swear in both the scales against either scale;
who committed treason enough for God's sake,
yet could not equivocate to heaven: O, come
in, equivocator.

Knocking within

Knock,
knock, knock! Who's there? Faith, here's an
English tailor come hither, for stealing out of
a French hose: come in, tailor; here you may
roast your goose.

Knocking within

Knock,
knock; never at quiet! What are you? But
this place is too cold for hell. I'll devil-porter
it no further: I had thought to have let in
some of all professions that go the primrose
way to the everlasting bonfire.

Knocking within

Anon, anon! I pray you, remember the porter.

Opens the gate

Enter MACDUFF and LENNOX

MACDUFF

Was it so late, friend, ere you went to bed,
That you do lie so late?

Porter

Faith sir, we were carousing till the
second cock: and drink, sir, is a great
provoker of three things.

MACDUFF

What three things does drink especially provoke?

Porter

Marry, sir, nose-painting, sleep, and
urine. Lechery, sir, it provokes, and unprovokes;
it provokes the desire, but it takes
away the performance: therefore, much drink
may be said to be an equivocator with lechery:
it makes him, and it mars him; it sets
him on, and it takes him off; it persuades him,
and disheartens him; makes him stand to, and
not stand to; in conclusion, equivocates him
in a sleep, and, giving him the lie, leaves him.

MACDUFF

I believe drink gave thee the lie last night.

Porter

That it did, sir, i' the very throat on
me: but I requited him for his lie; and, I

think, being too strong for him, though he took up my legs sometime, yet I made a shift to cast him.

MACDUFF

Is thy master stirring?

Enter MACBETH

Our knocking has awaked him; here he comes.

LENNOX

Good morrow, noble sir.

MACBETH

Good morrow, both.

MACDUFF

Is the king stirring, worthy thane?

MACBETH

Not yet.

MACDUFF

He did command me to call timely on him:
I have almost slipp'd the hour.

MACBETH

I'll bring you to him.

MACDUFF

I know this is a joyful trouble to you;
But yet 'tis one.

MACBETH

The labour we delight in physics pain.
This is the door.

MACDUFF

I'll make so bold to call,
For 'tis my limited service.

Exit

LENNOX

Goes the king hence to-day?

MACBETH

He does: he did appoint so.

LENNOX

The night has been unruly: where we lay,
Our chimneys were blown down; and, as they say,
Lamentings heard i' the air; strange screams of death,
And prophesying with accents terrible
Of dire combustion and confused events
New hatch'd to the woeful time: the obscure bird
Clamour'd the livelong night: some say, the earth
Was feverous and did shake.

MACBETH

'Twas a rough night.

LENNOX

My young remembrance cannot parallel
A fellow to it.

Re-enter MACDUFF

MACDUFF

O horror, horror, horror! Tongue nor heart
Cannot conceive nor name thee!

MACBETH LENNOX

What's the matter.

MACDUFF

Confusion now hath made his masterpiece!
Most sacrilegious murder hath broke ope
The Lord's anointed temple, and stole thence
The life o' the building!

MACBETH

What is 't you say? the life?

LENNOX

Mean you his majesty?

MACDUFF

Approach the chamber, and destroy your sight
With a new Gorgon: do not bid me speak;
See, and then speak yourselves.

Exeunt MACBETH and LENNOX

Awake, awake!
Ring the alarum-bell. Murder and treason!
Banquo and Donalbain! Malcolm! awake!
Shake off this downy sleep, death's counterfeit,
And look on death itself! up, up, and see
The great doom's image! Malcolm! Banquo!
As from your graves rise up, and walk like sprites,
To countenance this horror! Ring the bell.

Bell rings

Enter LADY MACBETH

LADY MACBETH

What's the business,
That such a hideous trumpet calls to parley
The sleepers of the house? speak, speak!

MACDUFF

O gentle lady,
'Tis not for you to hear what I can speak:
The repetition, in a woman's ear,
Would murder as it fell.

Enter BANQUO

O Banquo, Banquo,
Our royal master 's murder'd!

LADY MACBETH

Woe, alas!
What, in our house?

BANQUO

Too cruel any where.
Dear Duff, I prithee, contradict thyself,
And say it is not so.

Re-enter MACBETH and LENNOX, with ROSS

MACBETH

Had I but died an hour before this chance,
I had lived a blessed time; for, from this instant,
There 's nothing serious in mortality:

All is but toys: renown and grace is dead;
The wine of life is drawn, and the mere lees
Is left this vault to brag of.

Enter MALCOLM and DONALBAIN

DONALBAIN

What is amiss?

MACBETH

You are, and do not know't:
The spring, the head, the fountain of your blood
Is stopp'd; the very source of it is stopp'd.

MACDUFF

Your royal father 's murder'd.

MALCOLM

O, by whom?

LENNOX

Those of his chamber, as it seem'd, had done 't:
Their hands and faces were all badged with blood;
So were their daggers, which unwiped we found
Upon their pillows:
They stared, and were distracted; no man's life
Was to be trusted with them.

MACBETH

O, yet I do repent me of my fury,
That I did kill them.

MACDUFF

Wherefore did you so?

MACBETH

Who can be wise, amazed, temperate and furious,
Loyal and neutral, in a moment? No man:
The expedition my violent love
Outrun the pauser, reason. Here lay Duncan,
His silver skin laced with his golden blood;
And his gash'd stabs look'd like a breach in nature
For ruin's wasteful entrance: there, the murderers,
Steep'd in the colours of their trade, their daggers

Unmannerly breech'd with gore: who could refrain,
That had a heart to love, and in that heart
Courage to make 's love known?

LADY MACBETH

Help me hence, ho!

MACDUFF

Look to the lady.

MALCOLM

[Aside to DONALBAIN] Why do we hold our tongues,
That most may claim this argument for ours?

DONALBAIN

[Aside to MALCOLM] What should be spoken here, where our fate,
Hid in an auger-hole, may rush, and seize us?
Let 's away;
Our tears are not yet brew'd.

MALCOLM

[Aside to DONALBAIN] Nor our strong sorrow
Upon the foot of motion.

BANQUO

Look to the lady:
LADY MACBETH is carried out
And when we have our naked frailties hid,
That suffer in exposure, let us meet,
And question this most bloody piece of work,
To know it further. Fears and scruples shake us:
In the great hand of God I stand; and thence
Against the undivulged pretence I fight
Of treasonous malice.

MACDUFF

And so do I.

ALL

So all.

MACBETH

Let's briefly put on manly readiness,
And meet i' the hall together.

ALL

Well contented.

Exeunt all but Malcolm and Donalbain.

MALCOLM

What will you do? Let's not consort with them:
To show an unfelt sorrow is an office
Which the false man does easy. I'll to England.

DONALBAIN

To Ireland, I; our separated fortune
Shall keep us both the safer: where we are,
There's daggers in men's smiles: the near in blood,
The nearer bloody.

MALCOLM

This murderous shaft that's shot
Hath not yet lighted, and our safest way
Is to avoid the aim. Therefore, to horse;
And let us not be dainty of leave-taking,
But shift away: there's warrant in that theft
Which steals itself, when there's no mercy left.

Exeunt

SCENE IV. Outside Macbeth's castle

Enter ROSS and an old Man

Old Man

Threescore and ten I can remember well:
Within the volume of which time I have seen
Hours dreadful and things strange; but this sore night
Hath trifled former knowings.

ROSS

Ah, good father,
Thou seest, the heavens, as troubled with man's act,
Threaten his bloody stage: by the clock, 'tis day,
And yet dark night strangles the travelling lamp:
Is't night's predominance, or the day's shame,
That darkness does the face of earth entomb,
When living light should kiss it?

Old Man

'Tis unnatural,
Even like the deed that's done. On Tuesday last,
A falcon, towering in her pride of place,
Was by a mousing owl hawk'd at and kill'd.

ROSS

And Duncan's horses—a thing most strange and certain—
Beauteous and swift, the minions of their race,
Turn'd wild in nature, broke their stalls, flung out,
Contending 'gainst obedience, as they would make
War with mankind.

Old Man

'Tis said they eat each other.

ROSS

They did so, to the amazement of mine eyes
That look'd upon't. Here comes the good Macduff.

Enter MACDUFF

How goes the world, sir, now?

MACDUFF

Why, see you not?

ROSS

Is't known who did this more than bloody deed?

MACDUFF

Those that Macbeth hath slain.

ROSS

Alas, the day!
What good could they pretend?

MACDUFF

They were suborn'd:
Malcolm and Donalbain, the king's two sons,
Are stol'n away and fled; which puts upon them
Suspicion of the deed.

ROSS

'Gainst nature still!
Thriftless ambition, that wilt ravin up

Thine own life's means! Then 'tis most like
The sovereignty will fall upon Macbeth.

MACDUFF

He is already named, and gone to Scone
To be invested.

ROSS

Where is Duncan's body?

MACDUFF

Carried to Colmekill,
The sacred storehouse of his predecessors,
And guardian of their bones.

ROSS

Will you to Scone?

MACDUFF

No, cousin, I'll to Fife.

ROSS

Well, I will thither.

MACDUFF

Well, may you see things well done there: adieu!
Lest our old robes sit easier than our new!

ROSS

Farewell, father.

Old Man

God's benison go with you; and with those
That would make good or bad, and friends or foes!

Exeunt

ACT III

SCENE I. Forres. The Palace

Enter BANQUO

BANQUO

Thou hast it now: king, Cawdor, Glamis, all,
As the weird women promised, and, I fear,
Thou play'dst most foully for't: yet it was said

It should not stand in thy posterity,
But that myself should be the root and father
Of many kings. If there come truth from them—
As upon thee, Macbeth, their speeches shine—
Why, by the verities on thee made good,
May they not be my oracles as well,
And set me up in hope? But hush! no more.

Sennet sounded. Enter MACBETH, as king, LADY MACBETH, as queen, LENNOX, ROSS, Lords, Ladies, and Attendants

MACBETH

Here's our chief guest.

LADY MACBETH

If he had been forgotten,
It had been as a gap in our great feast,
And all-thing unbecoming.

MACBETH

To-night we hold a solemn supper sir,
And I'll request your presence.

BANQUO

Let your highness
Command upon me; to the which my duties
Are with a most indissoluble tie
For ever knit.

MACBETH

Ride you this afternoon?

BANQUO

Ay, my good lord.

MACBETH

We should have else desired your good advice,
Which still hath been both grave and prosperous,
In this day's council; but we'll take to-morrow.
Is't far you ride?

BANQUO

As far, my lord, as will fill up the time
'Twixt this and supper: go not my horse the better,

I must become a borrower of the night
For a dark hour or twain.

MACBETH

Fail not our feast.

BANQUO

My lord, I will not.

MACBETH

We hear, our bloody cousins are bestow'd
In England and in Ireland, not confessing
Their cruel parricide, filling their hearers
With strange invention: but of that to-morrow,
When therewithal we shall have cause of state
Craving us jointly. Hie you to horse: adieu,
Till you return at night. Goes Fleance with you?

BANQUO

Ay, my good lord: our time does call upon 's.

MACBETH

I wish your horses swift and sure of foot;
And so I do commend you to their backs. Farewell.

Exit

BANQUO

Let every man be master of his time
Till seven at night: to make society
The sweeter welcome, we will keep ourself
Till supper-time alone: while then, God be with you!

Exeunt all but MACBETH, and an attendant

Sirrah, a word with you: attend those men
Our pleasure?

ATTENDANT

They are, my lord, without the palace gate.

MACBETH

Bring them before us.

Exit Attendant

To be thus is nothing;
But to be safely thus.—Our fears in Banquo
Stick deep; and in his royalty of nature

Reigns that which would be fear'd: 'tis much he dares;
And, to that dauntless temper of his mind,
He hath a wisdom that doth guide his valour
To act in safety. There is none but he
Whose being I do fear: and, under him,
My Genius is rebuked; as, it is said,
Mark Antony's was by Caesar. He chid the sisters
When first they put the name of king upon me,
And bade them speak to him: then prophet-like
They hail'd him father to a line of kings:
Upon my head they placed a fruitless crown,
And put a barren sceptre in my gripe,
Thence to be wrench'd with an unlineal hand,
No son of mine succeeding. If 't be so,
For Banquo's issue have I filed my mind;
For them the gracious Duncan have I murder'd;
Put rancours in the vessel of my peace
Only for them; and mine eternal jewel
Given to the common enemy of man,
To make them kings, the seed of Banquo kings!
Rather than so, come fate into the list.
And champion me to the utterance! Who's there!
Re-enter Attendant, with two Murderers
Now go to the door, and stay there till we call.
Exit Attendant
Was it not yesterday we spoke together?

First Murderer

It was, so please your highness.

MACBETH

Well then, now
Have you consider'd of my speeches? Know
That it was he in the times past which held you
So under fortune, which you thought had been
Our innocent self: this I made good to you
In our last conference, pass'd in probation with you,
How you were borne in hand, how cross'd,
the instruments,

Who wrought with them, and all things else that might
To half a soul and to a notion crazed
Say "Thus did Banquo."

First Murderer

You made it known to us.

MACBETH

I did so, and went further, which is now
Our point of second meeting. Do you find
Your patience so predominant in your nature
That you can let this go? Are you so gospell'd
To pray for this good man and for his issue,
Whose heavy hand hath bow'd you to the grave
And beggar'd yours for ever?

First Murderer

We are men, my liege.

MACBETH

Ay, in the catalogue ye go for men;
As hounds and greyhounds, mongrels, spaniels, curs,
Shoughs, water-rugs and demi-wolves, are clept
All by the name of dogs: the valued file
Distinguishes the swift, the slow, the subtle,
The housekeeper, the hunter, every one
According to the gift which bounteous nature
Hath in him closed; whereby he does receive
Particular addition from the bill
That writes them all alike: and so of men.
Now, if you have a station in the file,
Not i' the worst rank of manhood, say 't;
And I will put that business in your bosoms,
Whose execution takes your enemy off,
Grapples you to the heart and love of us,
Who wear our health but sickly in his life,
Which in his death were perfect.

Second Murderer

I am one, my liege,
Whom the vile blows and buffets of the world

Have so incensed that I am reckless what
I do to spite the world.

First Murderer

And I another
So weary with disasters, tugg'd with fortune,
That I would set my lie on any chance,
To mend it, or be rid on't.

MACBETH

Both of you
Know Banquo was your enemy.

Both Murderers

True, my lord.

MACBETH

So is he mine; and in such bloody distance,
That every minute of his being thrusts
Against my near'st of life: and though I could
With barefaced power sweep him from my sight
And bid my will avouch it, yet I must not,
For certain friends that are both his and mine,
Whose loves I may not drop, but wail his fall
Who I myself struck down; and thence it is,
That I to your assistance do make love,
Masking the business from the common eye
For sundry weighty reasons.

Second Murderer

We shall, my lord
Perform what you command us.

First Murderer

Though our lives—

MACBETH

Your spirits shine through you. Within this hour at most
I will advise you where to plant yourselves;
Acquaint you with the perfect spy o' the time,
The moment on't; for't must be done to-night,
And something from the palace; always thought
That I require a clearness: and with him—

To leave no rubs nor botches in the work—
Fleance his son, that keeps him company,
Whose absence is no less material to me
Than is his father's, must embrace the fate
Of that dark hour. Resolve yourselves apart:
I'll come to you anon.

Both Murderers

We are resolved, my lord.

MACBETH

I'll call upon you straight: abide within.

Exeunt Murderers

It is concluded. Banquo, thy soul's flight,
If it find heaven, must find it out to-night.

Exit

SCENE II. The palace

Enter LADY MACBETH and a Servant

LADY MACBETH

Is Banquo gone from court?

Servant

Ay, madam, but returns again to-night.

LADY MACBETH

Say to the king, I would attend his leisure
For a few words.

Servant

Madam, I will.

Exit

LADY MACBETH

Nought's had, all's spent,
Where our desire is got without content:
'Tis safer to be that which we destroy
Than by destruction dwell in doubtful joy.

Enter MACBETH

How now, my lord! why do you keep alone,
Of sorriest fancies your companions making,

Using those thoughts which should indeed have died
With them they think on? Things without all remedy
Should be without regard: what's done is done.

MACBETH

We have scotch'd the snake, not kill'd it:
She'll close and be herself, whilst our poor malice
Remains in danger of her former tooth.
But let the frame of things disjoint, both the worlds suffer,
Ere we will eat our meal in fear and sleep
In the affliction of these terrible dreams
That shake us nightly: better be with the dead,
Whom we, to gain our peace, have sent to peace,
Than on the torture of the mind to lie
In restless ecstasy. Duncan is in his grave;
After life's fitful fever he sleeps well;
Treason has done his worst: nor steel, nor poison,
Malice domestic, foreign levy, nothing,
Can touch him further.

LADY MACBETH

Come on;
Gentle my lord, sleek o'er your rugged looks;
Be bright and jovial among your guests to-night.

MACBETH

So shall I, love; and so, I pray, be you:
Let your remembrance apply to Banquo;
Present him eminence, both with eye and tongue:
Unsafe the while, that we
Must lave our honours in these flattering streams,
And make our faces vizards to our hearts,
Disguising what they are.

LADY MACBETH

You must leave this.

MACBETH

O, full of scorpions is my mind, dear wife!
Thou know'st that Banquo, and his Fleance, lives.

LADY MACBETH

But in them nature's copy's not eterne.

MACBETH

There's comfort yet; they are assailable;
Then be thou jocund: ere the bat hath flown
His cloister'd flight, ere to black Hecate's summons
The shard-borne beetle with his drowsy hums
Hath rung night's yawning peal, there shall be done
A deed of dreadful note.

LADY MACBETH

What's to be done?

MACBETH

Be innocent of the knowledge, dearest chuck,
Till thou applaud the deed. Come, seeling night,
Scarf up the tender eye of pitiful day;
And with thy bloody and invisible hand
Cancel and tear to pieces that great bond
Which keeps me pale! Light thickens; and the crow
Makes wing to the rooky wood:
Good things of day begin to droop and drowse;
While night's black agents to their preys do rouse.
Thou marvell'st at my words: but hold thee still;
Things bad begun make strong themselves by ill.
So, prithee, go with me.

Exeunt

SCENE III. A Park near the Palace

Enter three Murderers

First Murderer

But who did bid thee join with us?

Third Murderer

Macbeth.

Second Murderer

He needs not our mistrust, since he delivers
Our offices and what we have to do
To the direction just.

First Murderer

Then stand with us.
The west yet glimmers with some streaks of day:
Now spurs the lated traveller apace
To gain the timely inn; and near approaches
The subject of our watch.

Third Murderer

Hark! I hear horses.

BANQUO

[Within] Give us a light there, ho!

Second Murderer

Then 'tis he: the rest
That are within the note of expectation
Already are i' the court.

First Murderer

His horses go about.

Third Murderer

Almost a mile: but he does usually,
So all men do, from hence to the palace gate
Make it their walk.

Second Murderer

A light, a light!

Enter BANQUO, and FLEANCE with a torch

Third Murderer

'Tis he.

First Murderer

Stand to't.

BANQUO

It will be rain to-night.

First Murderer

Let it come down.

They set upon BANQUO

BANQUO

O, treachery! Fly, good Fleance, fly, fly, fly!
Thou mayst revenge. O slave!

Dies. FLEANCE escapes

Third Murderer

Who did strike out the light?

First Murderer

Wast not the way?

Third Murderer

There's but one down; the son is fled.

Second Murderer

We have lost
Best half of our affair.

First Murderer

Well, let's away, and say how much is done.

Exeunt

SCENE IV. The same. Hall in the palace

A banquet prepared. Enter MACBETH, LADY MACBETH, ROSS, LENNOX, Lords, and Attendants

MACBETH

You know your own degrees; sit down: at first
And last the hearty welcome.

Lords

Thanks to your majesty.

MACBETH

Ourself will mingle with society,
And play the humble host.
Our hostess keeps her state, but in best time
We will require her welcome.

LADY MACBETH

Pronounce it for me, sir, to all our friends;
For my heart speaks they are welcome.

First Murderer appears at the door

MACBETH

See, they encounter thee with their hearts' thanks.
Both sides are even: here I'll sit i' the midst:
Be large in mirth; anon we'll drink a measure
The table round.

Approaching the door

There's blood on thy face.

First Murderer

'Tis Banquo's then.

MACBETH

'Tis better thee without than he within.
Is he dispatch'd?

First Murderer

My lord, his throat is cut; that I did for him.

MACBETH

Thou art the best o' the cut-throats: yet he's good
That did the like for Fleance: if thou didst it,
Thou art the nonpareil.

First Murderer

Most royal sir,
Fleance is 'scaped.

MACBETH

Then comes my fit again: I had else been perfect,
Whole as the marble, founded as the rock,
As broad and general as the casing air:
But now I am cabin'd, cribb'd, confined, bound in
To saucy doubts and fears. But Banquo's safe?

First Murderer

Ay, my good lord: safe in a ditch he bides,
With twenty trenched gashes on his head;
The least a death to nature.

MACBETH

Thanks for that:
There the grown serpent lies; the worm that's fled

Hath nature that in time will venom breed,
No teeth for the present. Get thee gone: to-morrow
We'll hear, ourselves, again.

Exit Murderer

LADY MACBETH

My royal lord,
You do not give the cheer: the feast is sold
That is not often vouch'd, while 'tis a-making,
'Tis given with welcome: to feed were best at home;
From thence the sauce to meat is ceremony;
Meeting were bare without it.

MACBETH

Sweet remembrancer!
Now, good digestion wait on appetite,
And health on both!

LENNOX

May't please your highness sit.

The GHOST OF BANQUO enters, and sits in MACBETH's place

MACBETH

Here had we now our country's honour roof'd,
Were the graced person of our Banquo present;
Who may I rather challenge for unkindness
Than pity for mischance!

ROSS

His absence, sir,
Lays blame upon his promise. Please't your highness
To grace us with your royal company.

MACBETH

The table's full.

LENNOX

Here is a place reserved, sir.

MACBETH

Where?

LENNOX

Here, my good lord. What is't that moves your highness?

MACBETH

Which of you have done this?

Lords

What, my good lord?

MACBETH

Thou canst not say I did it: never shake
Thy gory locks at me.

ROSS

Gentlemen, rise: his highness is not well.

LADY MACBETH

Sit, worthy friends: my lord is often thus,
And hath been from his youth: pray you, keep seat;
The fit is momentary; upon a thought
He will again be well: if much you note him,
You shall offend him and extend his passion:
Feed, and regard him not. Are you a man?

MACBETH

Ay, and a bold one, that dare look on that
Which might appall the devil.

LADY MACBETH

O proper stuff!
This is the very painting of your fear:
This is the air-drawn dagger which, you said,
Led you to Duncan. O, these flaws and starts,
Impostors to true fear, would well become
A woman's story at a winter's fire,
Authorized by her grandam. Shame itself!
Why do you make such faces? When all's done,
You look but on a stool.

MACBETH

Prithee, see there! behold! look! lo!
how say you?
Why, what care I? If thou canst nod, speak too.

If charnel-houses and our graves must send
Those that we bury back, our monuments
Shall be the maws of kites.

GHOST OF BANQUO vanishes

LADY MACBETH

What, quite unmann'd in folly?

MACBETH

If I stand here, I saw him.

LADY MACBETH

Fie, for shame!

MACBETH

Blood hath been shed ere now, i' the olden time,
Ere human statute purged the gentle weal;
Ay, and since too, murders have been perform'd
Too terrible for the ear: the times have been,
That, when the brains were out, the man would die,
And there an end; but now they rise again,
With twenty mortal murders on their crowns,
And push us from our stools: this is more strange
Than such a murder is.

LADY MACBETH

My worthy lord,
Your noble friends do lack you.

MACBETH

I do forget.
Do not muse at me, my most worthy friends,
I have a strange infirmity, which is nothing
To those that know me. Come, love and health to all;
Then I'll sit down. Give me some wine; fill full.
I drink to the general joy o' the whole table,
And to our dear friend Banquo, whom we miss;
Would he were here! to all, and him, we thirst,
And all to all.

Lords

Our duties, and the pledge.

Re-enter GHOST OF BANQUO

MACBETH

Avaunt! and quit my sight! let the earth hide thee!
Thy bones are marrowless, thy blood is cold;
Thou hast no speculation in those eyes
Which thou dost glare with!

LADY MACBETH

Think of this, good peers,
But as a thing of custom: 'tis no other;
Only it spoils the pleasure of the time.

MACBETH

What man dare, I dare:
Approach thou like the rugged Russian bear,
The arm'd rhinoceros, or the Hyrcan tiger;
Take any shape but that, and my firm nerves
Shall never tremble: or be alive again,
And dare me to the desert with thy sword;
If trembling I inhabit then, protest me
The baby of a girl. Hence, horrible shadow!
Unreal mockery, hence!

GHOST OF BANQUO vanishes

Why, so: being gone,
I am a man again. Pray you, sit still.

LADY MACBETH

You have displaced the mirth, broke the good meeting,
With most admired disorder.

MACBETH

Can such things be,
And overcome us like a summer's cloud,
Without our special wonder? You make me strange
Even to the disposition that I owe,
When now I think you can behold such sights,
And keep the natural ruby of your cheeks,
When mine is blanched with fear.

ROSS

What sights, my lord?

LADY MACBETH

I pray you, speak not; he grows worse and worse;
Question enrages him. At once, good night:
Stand not upon the order of your going,
But go at once.

LENNOX

Good night; and better health
Attend his majesty!

LADY MACBETH

A kind good night to all!

Exeunt all but MACBETH and LADY MACBETH

MACBETH

It will have blood; they say, blood will have blood:
Stones have been known to move and trees to speak;
Augurs and understood relations have
By magot-pies and choughs and rooks brought forth
The secret'st man of blood. What is the night?

LADY MACBETH

Almost at odds with morning, which is which.

MACBETH

How say'st thou, that Macduff denies his person
At our great bidding?

LADY MACBETH

Did you send to him, sir?

MACBETH

I hear it by the way; but I will send:
There's not a one of them but in his house
I keep a servant fee'd. I will to-morrow,
And betimes I will, to the weird sisters:
More shall they speak; for now I am bent to know,
By the worst means, the worst. For mine own good,
All causes shall give way: I am in blood
Stepp'd in so far that, should I wade no more,
Returning were as tedious as go o'er:
Strange things I have in head, that will to hand;
Which must be acted ere they may be scann'd.

LADY MACBETH

You lack the season of all natures, sleep.

MACBETH

Come, we'll to sleep. My strange and self-abuse
Is the initiate fear that wants hard use:
We are yet but young indeed.

Exeunt

SCENE V. A Heath

Thunder. Enter the three Witches meeting HECATE

First Witch

Why, how now, Hecate! you look angerly.

HECATE

Have I not reason, beldams as you are,
Saucy and overbold? How did you dare
To trade and traffic with Macbeth
In riddles and affairs of death;
And I, the mistress of your charms,
The close contriver of all harms,
Was never call'd to bear my part,
Or show the glory of our art?
And, which is worse, all you have done
Hath been but for a wayward son,
Spiteful and wrathful, who, as others do,
Loves for his own ends, not for you.
But make amends now: get you gone,
And at the pit of Acheron
Meet me i' the morning: thither he
Will come to know his destiny:
Your vessels and your spells provide,
Your charms and every thing beside.
I am for the air; this night I'll spend
Unto a dismal and a fatal end:
Great business must be wrought ere noon:
Upon the corner of the moon
There hangs a vaporous drop profound;
I'll catch it ere it come to ground:

And that distill'd by magic sleights
Shall raise such artificial sprites
As by the strength of their illusion
Shall draw him on to his confusion:
He shall spurn fate, scorn death, and bear
He hopes 'bove wisdom, grace and fear:
And you all know, security
Is mortals' chiefest enemy.

Music and a song within: 'Come away, come away,' &c

Hark! I am call'd; my little spirit, see,
Sits in a foggy cloud, and stays for me.

Exit

First Witch

Come, let's make haste; she'll soon be back again.

Exeunt

SCENE VI. Forres. The Palace

Enter LENNOX and another Lord

LENNOX

My former speeches have but hit your thoughts,
Which can interpret further: only, I say,
Things have been strangely borne. The
gracious Duncan
Was pitied of Macbeth: marry, he was dead:
And the right-valiant Banquo walk'd too late;
Whom, you may say, if't please you, Fleance kill'd,
For Fleance fled: men must not walk too late.
Who cannot want the thought how monstrous
It was for Malcolm and for Donalbain
To kill their gracious father? damned fact!
How it did grieve Macbeth! did he not straight
In pious rage the two delinquents tear,
That were the slaves of drink and thralls of sleep?
Was not that nobly done? Ay, and wisely too;
For 'twould have anger'd any heart alive
To hear the men deny't. So that, I say,
He has borne all things well: and I do think

That had he Duncan's sons under his key—
As, an't please heaven, he shall not—they
should find
What 'twere to kill a father; so should Fleance.
But, peace! for from broad words and 'cause he fail'd
His presence at the tyrant's feast, I hear
Macduff lives in disgrace: sir, can you tell
Where he bestows himself?

Lord

The son of Duncan,
From whom this tyrant holds the due of birth
Lives in the English court, and is received
Of the most pious Edward with such grace
That the malevolence of fortune nothing
Takes from his high respect: thither Macduff
Is gone to pray the holy king, upon his aid
To wake Northumberland and warlike Siward:
That, by the help of these—with Him above
To ratify the work—we may again
Give to our tables meat, sleep to our nights,
Free from our feasts and banquets bloody knives,
Do faithful homage and receive free honours:
All which we pine for now: and this report
Hath so exasperate the king that he
Prepares for some attempt of war.

LENNOX

Sent he to Macduff?

Lord

He did: and with an absolute 'Sir, not I,'
The cloudy messenger turns me his back,
And hums, as who should say "You'll rue the time
That clogs me with this answer."

LENNOX

And that well might
Advise him to a caution, to hold what distance
His wisdom can provide. Some holy angel
Fly to the court of England and unfold

His message ere he come, that a swift blessing
May soon return to this our suffering country
Under a hand accursed!

Lord

I'll send my prayers with him.

Exeunt

ACT IV

SCENE I. A Cavern. In the Middle, a Boiling Cauldron

Thunder. Enter the three Witches

First Witch

Thrice the brinded cat hath mew'd.

Second Witch

Thrice and once the hedge-pig whined.

Third Witch

Harpier cries 'Tis time, 'tis time.

First Witch

Round about the cauldron go;
In the poison'd entrails throw.
Toad, that under cold stone
Days and nights has thirty-one
Swelter'd venom sleeping got,
Boil thou first i' the charmed pot.

ALL

Double, double toil and trouble;
Fire burn, and cauldron bubble.

Second Witch

Fillet of a fenny snake,
In the cauldron boil and bake;
Eye of newt and toe of frog,
Wool of bat and tongue of dog,
Adder's fork and blind-worm's sting,
Lizard's leg and owlet's wing,
For a charm of powerful trouble,
Like a hell-broth boil and bubble.

ALL

Double, double toil and trouble;
Fire burn and cauldron bubble.

Third Witch

Scale of dragon, tooth of wolf,
Witches' mummy, maw and gulf
Of the ravin'd salt-sea shark,
Root of hemlock digg'd i' the dark,
Liver of blaspheming Jew,
Gall of goat, and slips of yew
Silver'd in the moon's eclipse,
Nose of Turk and Tartar's lips,
Finger of birth-strangled babe
Ditch-deliver'd by a drab,
Make the gruel thick and slab:
Add thereto a tiger's chaudron,
For the ingredients of our cauldron.

ALL

Double, double toil and trouble;
Fire burn and cauldron bubble.

Second Witch

Cool it with a baboon's blood,
Then the charm is firm and good.

Enter HECATE to the other three Witches

HECATE

O well done! I commend your pains;
And every one shall share i' the gains;
And now about the cauldron sing,
Live elves and fairies in a ring,
Enchanting all that you put in.

Music and a song: 'Black spirits,' &c

HECATE retires

Second Witch

By the pricking of my thumbs,
Something wicked this way comes.

Open, locks,
Whoever knocks!

Enter MACBETH

MACBETH

How now, you secret, black, and midnight hags!
What is't you do?

ALL

A deed without a name.

MACBETH

I conjure you, by that which you profess,
Howe'er you come to know it, answer me:
Though you untie the winds and let them fight
Against the churches; though the yesty waves
Confound and swallow navigation up;
Though bladed corn be lodged and trees blown down;
Though castles topple on their warders' heads;
Though palaces and pyramids do slope
Their heads to their foundations; though the treasure
Of nature's germens tumble all together,
Even till destruction sicken; answer me
To what I ask you.

First Witch

Speak.

Second Witch

Demand.

Third Witch

We'll answer.

First Witch

Say, if thou'dst rather hear it from our mouths,
Or from our masters?

MACBETH

Call 'em; let me see 'em.

First Witch

Pour in sow's blood, that hath eaten
Her nine farrow; grease that's sweaten

From the murderer's gibbet throw
Into the flame.

ALL

Come, high or low;
Thyself and office deftly show!

Thunder. First Apparition: an armed Head

MACBETH

Tell me, thou unknown power,—

First Witch

He knows thy thought:
Hear his speech, but say thou nought.

First Apparition

Macbeth! Macbeth! Macbeth! beware Macduff;
Beware the thane of Fife. Dismiss me. Enough.

Descends

MACBETH

Whate'er thou art, for thy good caution, thanks;
Thou hast harp'd my fear aright: but one
word more,—

First Witch

He will not be commanded: here's another,
More potent than the first.

Thunder. Second Apparition: A bloody Child

Second Apparition

Macbeth! Macbeth! Macbeth!

MACBETH

Had I three ears, I'ld hear thee.

Second Apparition

Be bloody, bold, and resolute; laugh to scorn
The power of man, for none of woman born
Shall harm Macbeth.

Descends

MACBETH

Then live, Macduff: what need I fear of thee?
But yet I'll make assurance double sure,

And take a bond of fate: thou shalt not live;
That I may tell pale-hearted fear it lies,
And sleep in spite of thunder.

Thunder. Third Apparition: a Child crowned, with a tree in his hand

What is this
That rises like the issue of a king,
And wears upon his baby-brow the round
And top of sovereignty?

ALL

Listen, but speak not to't.

Third Apparition

Be lion-mettled, proud; and take no care
Who chafes, who frets, or where conspirers are:
Macbeth shall never vanquish'd be until
Great Birnam Wood to high Dunsinane hill
Shall come against him.

Descends

MACBETH

That will never be
Who can impress the forest, bid the tree
Unfix his earth-bound root? Sweet bodements! good!
Rebellion's head, rise never till the wood
Of Birnam rise, and our high-placed Macbeth
Shall live the lease of nature, pay his breath
To time and mortal custom. Yet my heart
Throbs to know one thing: tell me, if your art
Can tell so much: shall Banquo's issue ever
Reign in this kingdom?

ALL

Seek to know no more.

MACBETH

I will be satisfied: deny me this,
And an eternal curse fall on you! Let me know.
Why sinks that cauldron? and what noise is this?

Hautboys

First Witch

Show!

Second Witch

Show!

Third Witch

Show!

ALL

Show his eyes, and grieve his heart;
Come like shadows, so depart!

A show of Eight Kings, the last with a glass in his hand; GHOST OF BANQUO following

MACBETH

Thou art too like the spirit of Banquo: down!
Thy crown does sear mine eye-balls. And thy hair,
Thou other gold-bound brow, is like the first.
A third is like the former. Filthy hags!
Why do you show me this? A fourth! Start, eyes!
What, will the line stretch out to the crack of doom?
Another yet! A seventh! I'll see no more:
And yet the eighth appears, who bears a glass
Which shows me many more; and some I see
That two-fold balls and treble scepters carry:
Horrible sight! Now, I see, 'tis true;
For the blood-bolter'd Banquo smiles upon me,
And points at them for his.

What? is this so?

First Witch

Ay, sir, all this is so: but why
Stands Macbeth thus amazedly?
Come, sisters, cheer we up his sprites,
And show the best of our delights:
I'll charm the air to give a sound,
While you perform your antic round:
That this great king may kindly say,
Our duties did his welcome pay.

Music. The witches dance and then vanish, with HECATE

MACBETH

Where are they? Gone? Let this pernicious hour
Stand aye accursed in the calendar!
Come in, without there!

Enter LENNOX

LENNOX

What's your grace's will?

MACBETH

Saw you the weird sisters?

LENNOX

No, my lord.

MACBETH

Came they not by you?

LENNOX

No, indeed, my lord.

MACBETH

Infected be the air whereon they ride;
And damn'd all those that trust them! I did hear
The galloping of horse: who was't came by?

LENNOX

'Tis two or three, my lord, that bring you word
Macduff is fled to England.

MACBETH

Fled to England!

LENNOX

Ay, my good lord.

MACBETH

Time, thou anticipatest my dread exploits:
The flighty purpose never is o'ertook
Unless the deed go with it; from this moment
The very firstlings of my heart shall be
The firstlings of my hand. And even now,
To crown my thoughts with acts, be it thought and done:

The castle of Macduff I will surprise;
Seize upon Fife; give to the edge o' the sword
His wife, his babes, and all unfortunate souls
That trace him in his line. No boasting like a fool;
This deed I'll do before this purpose cool.
But no more sights!—Where are these gentlemen?
Come, bring me where they are.
Exeunt

SCENE II. Fife. Macduff's castle

Enter LADY MACDUFF, her Son, and ROSS

LADY MACDUFF

What had he done, to make him fly the land?

ROSS

You must have patience, madam.

LADY MACDUFF

He had none:
His flight was madness: when our actions do not,
Our fears do make us traitors.

ROSS

You know not
Whether it was his wisdom or his fear.

LADY MACDUFF

Wisdom! to leave his wife, to leave his babes,
His mansion and his titles in a place
From whence himself does fly? He loves us not;
He wants the natural touch: for the poor wren,
The most diminutive of birds, will fight,
Her young ones in her nest, against the owl.
All is the fear and nothing is the love;
As little is the wisdom, where the flight
So runs against all reason.

ROSS

My dearest coz,
I pray you, school yourself: but for your husband,
He is noble, wise, judicious, and best knows

The fits o' the season. I dare not speak
much further;
But cruel are the times, when we are traitors
And do not know ourselves, when we hold rumour
From what we fear, yet know not what we fear,
But float upon a wild and violent sea
Each way and move. I take my leave of you:
Shall not be long but I'll be here again:
Things at the worst will cease, or else climb upward
To what they were before. My pretty cousin,
Blessing upon you!

LADY MACDUFF

Father'd he is, and yet he's fatherless.

ROSS

I am so much a fool, should I stay longer,
It would be my disgrace and your discomfort:
I take my leave at once.

Exit

LADY MACDUFF

Sirrah, your father's dead;
And what will you do now? How will you live?

Son

As birds do, mother.

LADY MACDUFF

What, with worms and flies?

Son

With what I get, I mean; and so do they.

LADY MACDUFF

Poor bird! Thou'ldst never fear the net nor lime,
The pitfall nor the gin.

Son

Why should I, mother? Poor birds they are not set for.
My father is not dead, for all your saying.

LADY MACDUFF

Yes, he is dead; how wilt thou do for a father?

Son

Nay, how will you do for a husband?

LADY MACDUFF

Why, I can buy me twenty at any market.

Son

Then you'll buy 'em to sell again.

LADY MACDUFF

Thou speak'st with all thy wit: and yet, i' faith,
With wit enough for thee.

Son

Was my father a traitor, mother?

LADY MACDUFF

Ay, that he was.

Son

What is a traitor?

LADY MACDUFF

Why, one that swears and lies.

Son

And be all traitors that do so?

LADY MACDUFF

Every one that does so is a traitor, and must be hanged.

Son

And must they all be hanged that swear and lie?

LADY MACDUFF

Every one.

Son

Who must hang them?

LADY MACDUFF

Why, the honest men.

Son

Then the liars and swearers are fools,
for there are liars and swearers enough to beat
the honest men and hang up them.

LADY MACDUFF

Now, God help thee, poor monkey!
But how wilt thou do for a father?

Son

If he were dead, you'ld weep for
him: if you would not, it were a good sign
that I should quickly have a new father.

LADY MACDUFF

Poor prattler, how thou talk'st!

Enter a Messenger

Messenger

Bless you, fair dame! I am not to you known,
Though in your state of honour I am perfect.
I doubt some danger does approach you nearly:
If you will take a homely man's advice,
Be not found here; hence, with your little ones.
To fright you thus, methinks, I am too savage;
To do worse to you were fell cruelty,
Which is too nigh your person. Heaven preserve you!
I dare abide no longer.

Exit

LADY MACDUFF

Whither should I fly?
I have done no harm. But I remember now
I am in this earthly world; where to do harm
Is often laudable, to do good sometime
Accounted dangerous folly: why then, alas,
Do I put up that womanly defence,
To say I have done no harm?

Enter Murderers

What are these faces?

First Murderer

Where is your husband?

LADY MACDUFF

I hope, in no place so unsanctified
Where such as thou mayst find him.

First Murderer

He's a traitor.

Son

Thou liest, thou shag-hair'd villain!

First Murderer

What, you egg!

Stabbing him

Young fry of treachery!

Son

He has kill'd me, mother:
Run away, I pray you!

Dies

Exit LADY MACDUFF, crying 'Murder!' Exeunt Murderers, following her

SCENE III. England. Before the King's Palace

Enter MALCOLM and MACDUFF

MALCOLM

Let us seek out some desolate shade, and there
Weep our sad bosoms empty.

MACDUFF

Let us rather
Hold fast the mortal sword, and like good men
Bestride our down-fall'n birthdom: each new morn
New widows howl, new orphans cry, new sorrows
Strike heaven on the face, that it resounds
As if it felt with Scotland and yell'd out
Like syllable of dolour.

MALCOLM

What I believe I'll wail,
What know believe, and what I can redress,
As I shall find the time to friend, I will.
What you have spoke, it may be so perchance.
This tyrant, whose sole name blisters our tongues,
Was once thought honest: you have loved him well.

He hath not touch'd you yet. I am young;
but something
You may deserve of him through me, and wisdom
To offer up a weak poor innocent lamb
To appease an angry god.

MACDUFF

I am not treacherous.

MALCOLM

But Macbeth is.
A good and virtuous nature may recoil
In an imperial charge. But I shall crave
your pardon;
That which you are my thoughts cannot transpose:
Angels are bright still, though the brightest fell;
Though all things foul would wear the brows of grace,
Yet grace must still look so.

MACDUFF

I have lost my hopes.

MALCOLM

Perchance even there where I did find my doubts.
Why in that rawness left you wife and child,
Those precious motives, those strong knots of love,
Without leave-taking? I pray you,
Let not my jealousies be your dishonours,
But mine own safeties. You may be rightly just,
Whatever I shall think.

MACDUFF

Bleed, bleed, poor country!
Great tyranny! lay thou thy basis sure,
For goodness dare not check thee: wear thou
thy wrongs;
The title is affeer'd! Fare thee well, lord:
I would not be the villain that thou think'st
For the whole space that's in the tyrant's grasp,
And the rich East to boot.

MALCOLM

Be not offended:
I speak not as in absolute fear of you.
I think our country sinks beneath the yoke;
It weeps, it bleeds; and each new day a gash
Is added to her wounds: I think withal
There would be hands uplifted in my right;
And here from gracious England have I offer
Of goodly thousands: but, for all this,
When I shall tread upon the tyrant's head,
Or wear it on my sword, yet my poor country
Shall have more vices than it had before,
More suffer and more sundry ways than ever,
By him that shall succeed.

MACDUFF

What should he be?

MALCOLM

It is myself I mean: in whom I know
All the particulars of vice so grafted
That, when they shall be open'd, black Macbeth
Will seem as pure as snow, and the poor state
Esteem him as a lamb, being compared
With my confineless harms.

MACDUFF

Not in the legions
Of horrid hell can come a devil more damn'd
In evils to top Macbeth.

MALCOLM

I grant him bloody,
Luxurious, avaricious, false, deceitful,
Sudden, malicious, smacking of every sin
That has a name: but there's no bottom, none,
In my voluptuousness: your wives, your daughters,
Your matrons and your maids, could not fill up
The cistern of my lust, and my desire
All continent impediments would o'erbear

That did oppose my will: better Macbeth
Than such an one to reign.

MACDUFF

Boundless intemperance
In nature is a tyranny; it hath been
The untimely emptying of the happy throne
And fall of many kings. But fear not yet
To take upon you what is yours: you may
Convey your pleasures in a spacious plenty,
And yet seem cold, the time you may so hoodwink.
We have willing dames enough: there cannot be
That vulture in you, to devour so many
As will to greatness dedicate themselves,
Finding it so inclined.

MALCOLM

With this there grows
In my most ill-composed affection such
A stanchless avarice that, were I king,
I should cut off the nobles for their lands,
Desire his jewels and this other's house:
And my more-having would be as a sauce
To make me hunger more; that I should forge
Quarrels unjust against the good and loyal,
Destroying them for wealth.

MACDUFF

This avarice
Sticks deeper, grows with more pernicious root
Than summer-seeming lust, and it hath been
The sword of our slain kings: yet do not fear;
Scotland hath foisons to fill up your will.
Of your mere own: all these are portable,
With other graces weigh'd.

MALCOLM

But I have none: the king-becoming graces,
As justice, verity, temperance, stableness,
Bounty, perseverance, mercy, lowliness,
Devotion, patience, courage, fortitude,

I have no relish of them, but abound
In the division of each several crime,
Acting it many ways. Nay, had I power, I should
Pour the sweet milk of concord into hell,
Uproar the universal peace, confound
All unity on earth.

MACDUFF

O Scotland, Scotland!

MALCOLM

If such a one be fit to govern, speak:
I am as I have spoken.

MACDUFF

Fit to govern!
No, not to live. O nation miserable,
With an untitled tyrant bloody-scepter'd,
When shalt thou see thy wholesome days again,
Since that the truest issue of thy throne
By his own interdiction stands accursed,
And does blaspheme his breed? Thy royal father
Was a most sainted king: the queen that bore thee,
Oftener upon her knees than on her feet,
Died every day she lived. Fare thee well!
These evils thou repeat'st upon thyself
Have banish'd me from Scotland. O my breast,
Thy hope ends here!

MALCOLM

Macduff, this noble passion,
Child of integrity, hath from my soul
Wiped the black scruples, reconciled my thoughts
To thy good truth and honour. Devilish Macbeth
By many of these trains hath sought to win me
Into his power, and modest wisdom plucks me
From over-credulous haste: but God above
Deal between thee and me! for even now
I put myself to thy direction, and
Unspeak mine own detraction, here abjure
The taints and blames I laid upon myself,

For strangers to my nature. I am yet
Unknown to woman, never was forsworn,
Scarcely have coveted what was mine own,
At no time broke my faith, would not betray
The devil to his fellow and delight
No less in truth than life: my first false speaking
Was this upon myself: what I am truly,
Is thine and my poor country's to command:
Whither indeed, before thy here-approach,
Old Siward, with ten thousand warlike men,
Already at a point, was setting forth.
Now we'll together; and the chance of goodness
Be like our warranted quarrel! Why are you silent?

MACDUFF

Such welcome and unwelcome things at once
'Tis hard to reconcile.

Enter a Doctor

MALCOLM

Well; more anon.—Comes the king forth, I pray you?

Doctor

Ay, sir; there are a crew of wretched souls
That stay his cure: their malady convinces
The great assay of art; but at his touch—
Such sanctity hath heaven given his hand—
They presently amend.

MALCOLM

I thank you, doctor.

Exit Doctor

MACDUFF

What's the disease he means?

MALCOLM

'Tis call'd the evil:
A most miraculous work in this good king;
Which often, since my here-remain in England,
I have seen him do. How he solicits heaven,

Himself best knows: but strangely-visited people,
All swoln and ulcerous, pitiful to the eye,
The mere despair of surgery, he cures,
Hanging a golden stamp about their necks,
Put on with holy prayers: and 'tis spoken,
To the succeeding royalty he leaves
The healing benediction. With this strange virtue,
He hath a heavenly gift of prophecy,
And sundry blessings hang about his throne,
That speak him full of grace.

Enter ROSS

MACDUFF

See, who comes here?

MALCOLM

My countryman; but yet I know him not.

MACDUFF

My ever-gentle cousin, welcome hither.

MALCOLM

I know him now. Good God, betimes remove
The means that makes us strangers!

ROSS

Sir, amen.

MACDUFF

Stands Scotland where it did?

ROSS

Alas, poor country!
Almost afraid to know itself. It cannot
Be call'd our mother, but our grave; where nothing,
But who knows nothing, is once seen to smile;
Where sighs and groans and shrieks that rend the air
Are made, not mark'd; where violent sorrow seems
A modern ecstasy; the dead man's knell
Is there scarce ask'd for who; and good men's lives
Expire before the flowers in their caps,
Dying or ere they sicken.

MACDUFF

O, relation
Too nice, and yet too true!

MALCOLM

What's the newest grief?

ROSS

That of an hour's age doth hiss the speaker:
Each minute teems a new one.

MACDUFF

How does my wife?

ROSS

Why, well.

MACDUFF

And all my children?

ROSS

Well too.

MACDUFF

The tyrant has not batter'd at their peace?

ROSS

No; they were well at peace when I did leave 'em.

MACDUFF

But not a niggard of your speech: how goes't?

ROSS

When I came hither to transport the tidings,
Which I have heavily borne, there ran a rumour
Of many worthy fellows that were out;
Which was to my belief witness'd the rather,
For that I saw the tyrant's power a-foot:
Now is the time of help; your eye in Scotland
Would create soldiers, make our women fight,
To doff their dire distresses.

MALCOLM

Be't their comfort
We are coming thither: gracious England hath

Lent us good Siward and ten thousand men;
An older and a better soldier none
That Christendom gives out.

ROSS

Would I could answer
This comfort with the like! But I have words
That would be howl'd out in the desert air,
Where hearing should not latch them.

MACDUFF

What concern they?
The general cause? or is it a fee-grief
Due to some single breast?

ROSS

No mind that's honest
But in it shares some woe; though the main part
Pertains to you alone.

MACDUFF

If it be mine,
Keep it not from me, quickly let me have it.

ROSS

Let not your ears despise my tongue for ever,
Which shall possess them with the heaviest sound
That ever yet they heard.

MACDUFF

Hum! I guess at it.

ROSS

Your castle is surprised; your wife and babes
Savagely slaughter'd: to relate the manner,
Were, on the quarry of these murder'd deer,
To add the death of you.

MALCOLM

Merciful heaven!
What, man! Ne'er pull your hat upon your brows;
Give sorrow words: the grief that does not speak
Whispers the o'er-fraught heart and bids it break.

MACDUFF

My children too?

ROSS

Wife, children, servants, all
That could be found.

MACDUFF

And I must be from thence!
My wife kill'd too?

ROSS

I have said.

MALCOLM

Be comforted:
Let's make us medicines of our great revenge,
To cure this deadly grief.

MACDUFF

He has no children. All my pretty ones?
Did you say all? O hell-kite! All?
What, all my pretty chickens and their dam
At one fell swoop?

MALCOLM

Dispute it like a man.

MACDUFF

I shall do so;
But I must also feel it as a man:
I cannot but remember such things were,
That were most precious to me. Did heaven look on,
And would not take their part? Sinful Macduff,
They were all struck for thee! naught that I am,
Not for their own demerits, but for mine,
Fell slaughter on their souls. Heaven rest them now!

MALCOLM

Be this the whetstone of your sword: let grief
Convert to anger; blunt not the heart, enrage it.

MACDUFF

O, I could play the woman with mine eyes
And braggart with my tongue! But, gentle heavens,

Cut short all intermission; front to front
Bring thou this fiend of Scotland and myself;
Within my sword's length set him; if he 'scape,
Heaven forgive him too!

MALCOLM

This tune goes manly.
Come, go we to the king; our power is ready;
Our lack is nothing but our leave; Macbeth
Is ripe for shaking, and the powers above
Put on their instruments. Receive what cheer you may:
The night is long that never finds the day.
Exeunt

ACT V

SCENE I. Dunsinane. Ante-room in the castle

Enter a Doctor of Physic and a Waiting-Gentlewoman

Doctor

I have two nights watched with you, but can perceive no truth in your report. When was it she last walked?

Gentlewoman

Since his majesty went into the field, I have seen her rise from her bed, throw her night-gown upon her, unlock her closet, take forth paper, fold it, write upon't, read it, afterwards seal it, and again return to bed; yet all this while in a most fast sleep.

Doctor

A great perturbation in nature, to receive at once the benefit of sleep, and do the effects of watching! In this slumbery agitation, besides her walking and other actual performances, what, at any time, have you heard her say?

Gentlewoman

That, sir, which I will not report after her.

Doctor

You may to me: and 'tis most meet you should.

Gentlewoman

Neither to you nor any one; having no witness to confirm my speech.

Enter LADY MACBETH, with a taper

Lo you, here she comes! This is her very guise; and, upon my life, fast asleep. Observe her; stand close.

Doctor

How came she by that light?

Gentlewoman

Why, it stood by her: she has light by her continually; 'tis her command.

Doctor

You see, her eyes are open.

Gentlewoman

Ay, but their sense is shut.

Doctor

What is it she does now? Look, how she rubs her hands.

Gentlewoman

It is an accustomed action with her, to seem thus washing her hands: I have known her continue in this a quarter of an hour.

LADY MACBETH

Yet here's a spot.

Doctor

Hark! she speaks: I will set down what comes from her, to satisfy my remembrance the more strongly.

LADY MACBETH

Out, damned spot! out, I say!—One: two: why, then, 'tis time to do't.—Hell is murky!—Fie, my lord, fie! a soldier, and afeard? What need we fear who knows it, when none can call our power to account?—Yet who would have thought the old man to have had so much blood in him.

Doctor

Do you mark that?

LADY MACBETH

The thane of Fife had a wife: where is she now?—
What, will these hands ne'er be clean?—No more o'
that, my lord, no more o' that: you mar all with
this starting.

Doctor

Go to, go to; you have known what you should not.

Gentlewoman

She has spoke what she should not, I am sure of
that: heaven knows what she has known.

LADY MACBETH

Here's the smell of the blood still: all the
perfumes of Arabia will not sweeten this little
hand. Oh, oh, oh!

Doctor

What a sigh is there! The heart is sorely charged.

Gentlewoman

I would not have such a heart in my bosom for the
dignity of the whole body.

Doctor

Well, well, well,—

Gentlewoman

Pray God it be, sir.

Doctor

This disease is beyond my practise: yet I have known
those which have walked in their sleep who have died
holily in their beds.

LADY MACBETH

Wash your hands, put on your nightgown; look not so
pale.—I tell you yet again, Banquo's buried; he
cannot come out on's grave.

Doctor

Even so?

LADY MACBETH

To bed, to bed! There's knocking at the gate:
come, come, come, come, give me your hand. What's
done cannot be undone.—To bed, to bed, to bed!

Exit

Doctor

Will she go now to bed?

Gentlewoman

Directly.

Doctor

Foul whisperings are abroad: unnatural deeds
Do breed unnatural troubles: infected minds
To their deaf pillows will discharge their secrets:
More needs she the divine than the physician.
God, God forgive us all! Look after her;
Remove from her the means of all annoyance,
And still keep eyes upon her. So, good night:
My mind she has mated, and amazed my sight.
I think, but dare not speak.

Gentlewoman

Good night, good doctor.

Exeunt

SCENE II. The Country near Dunsinane

Drum and colours. Enter MENTEITH, CAITHNESS, ANGUS, LENNOX, and Soldiers

MENTEITH

The English power is near, led on by Malcolm,
His uncle Siward and the good Macduff:
Revenges burn in them; for their dear causes
Would to the bleeding and the grim alarm
Excite the mortified man.

ANGUS

Near Birnam Wood
Shall we well meet them; that way are they coming.

CAITHNESS

Who knows if Donalbain be with his brother?

LENNOX

For certain, sir, he is not: I have a file
Of all the gentry: there is Siward's son,
And many unrough youths that even now
Protest their first of manhood.

MENTEITH

What does the tyrant?

CAITHNESS

Great Dunsinane he strongly fortifies:
Some say he's mad; others that lesser hate him
Do call it valiant fury: but, for certain,
He cannot buckle his distemper'd cause
Within the belt of rule.

ANGUS

Now does he feel
His secret murders sticking on his hands;
Now minutely revolts upbraid his faith-breach;
Those he commands move only in command,
Nothing in love: now does he feel his title
Hang loose about him, like a giant's robe
Upon a dwarfish thief.

MENTEITH

Who then shall blame
His pester'd senses to recoil and start,
When all that is within him does condemn
Itself for being there?

CAITHNESS

Well, march we on,
To give obedience where 'tis truly owed:
Meet we the medicine of the sickly weal,

And with him pour we in our country's purge
Each drop of us.

LENNOX

Or so much as it needs,
To dew the sovereign flower and drown the weeds.
Make we our march towards Birnam.

Exeunt, marching

SCENE III. Dunsinane. A Room in the Castle

Enter MACBETH, Doctor, and Attendants

MACBETH

Bring me no more reports; let them fly all:
Till Birnam Wood remove to Dunsinane,
I cannot taint with fear. What's the boy Malcolm?
Was he not born of woman? The spirits that know
All mortal consequences have pronounced me thus:
"Fear not, Macbeth; no man that's born of woman
Shall e'er have power upon thee." Then fly,
false thanes,
And mingle with the English epicures:
The mind I sway by and the heart I bear
Shall never sag with doubt nor shake with fear.

Enter a Servant

The devil damn thee black, thou cream-faced loon!
Where got'st thou that goose look?

Servant

There is ten thousand—

MACBETH

Geese, villain!

Servant

Soldiers, sir.

MACBETH

Go prick thy face, and over-red thy fear,
Thou lily-liver'd boy. What soldiers, patch?
Death of thy soul! those linen cheeks of thine
Are counsellors to fear. What soldiers, whey-face?

Servant

The English force, so please you.

MACBETH

Take thy face hence.

Exit Servant

Seyton!—I am sick at heart,
When I behold—Seyton, I say!—This push
Will cheer me ever, or disseat me now.
I have lived long enough: my way of life
Is fall'n into the sear, the yellow leaf;
And that which should accompany old age,
As honour, love, obedience, troops of friends,
I must not look to have; but, in their stead,
Curses, not loud but deep, mouth-honour, breath,
Which the poor heart would fain deny, and dare not.
Seyton!

Enter SEYTON

SEYTON

What is your gracious pleasure?

MACBETH

What news more?

SEYTON

All is confirm'd, my lord, which was reported.

MACBETH

I'll fight till from my bones my flesh be hack'd.
Give me my armour.

SEYTON

'Tis not needed yet.

MACBETH

I'll put it on.
Send out more horses; skirr the country round;
Hang those that talk of fear. Give me mine armour.
How does your patient, doctor?

Doctor

Not so sick, my lord,
As she is troubled with thick coming fancies,
That keep her from her rest.

MACBETH

Cure her of that.
Canst thou not minister to a mind diseased,
Pluck from the memory a rooted sorrow,
Raze out the written troubles of the brain
And with some sweet oblivious antidote
Cleanse the stuff'd bosom of that perilous stuff
Which weighs upon the heart?

Doctor

Therein the patient
Must minister to himself.

MACBETH

Throw physic to the dogs; I'll none of it.
Come, put mine armour on; give me my staff.
Seyton, send out. Doctor, the thanes fly from me.
Come, sir, dispatch. If thou couldst, doctor, cast
The water of my land, find her disease,
And purge it to a sound and pristine health,
I would applaud thee to the very echo,
That should applaud again.—Pull't off, I say.—
What rhubarb, cyme, or what purgative drug,
Would scour these English hence? Hear'st thou of them?

Doctor

Ay, my good lord; your royal preparation
Makes us hear something.

MACBETH

Bring it after me.
I will not be afraid of death and bane,
Till Birnam forest come to Dunsinane.

Doctor

[Aside] Were I from Dunsinane away and clear,
Profit again should hardly draw me here.
Exeunt

SCENE IV. Country near Birnam Wood

Drum and colours. Enter MALCOLM, SIWARD and YOUNG SIWARD, MACDUFF, MENTEITH, CAITHNESS, ANGUS, LENNOX, ROSS, and Soldiers, marching

MALCOLM

Cousins, I hope the days are near at hand
That chambers will be safe.

MENTEITH

We doubt it nothing.

SIWARD

What wood is this before us?

MENTEITH

The wood of Birnam.

MALCOLM

Let every soldier hew him down a bough
And bear't before him: thereby shall we shadow
The numbers of our host and make discovery
Err in report of us.

Soldiers

It shall be done.

SIWARD

We learn no other but the confident tyrant
Keeps still in Dunsinane, and will endure
Our setting down before 't.

MALCOLM

'Tis his main hope:
For where there is advantage to be given,
Both more and less have given him the revolt,
And none serve with him but constrained things
Whose hearts are absent too.

MACDUFF

Let our just censures
Attend the true event, and put we on
Industrious soldiership.

SIWARD

The time approaches
That will with due decision make us know
What we shall say we have and what we owe.
Thoughts speculative their unsure hopes relate,
But certain issue strokes must arbitrate:
Towards which advance the war.

Exeunt, marching

SCENE V. Dunsinane. Within the Castle

Enter MACBETH, SEYTON, and Soldiers, with drum and colours

MACBETH

Hang out our banners on the outward walls;
The cry is still 'They come:' our castle's strength
Will laugh a siege to scorn: here let them lie
Till famine and the ague eat them up:
Were they not forced with those that should be ours,
We might have met them dareful, beard to beard,
And beat them backward home.

A cry of women within

What is that noise?

SEYTON

It is the cry of women, my good lord.

Exit

MACBETH

I have almost forgot the taste of fears;
The time has been, my senses would have cool'd
To hear a night-shriek; and my fell of hair
Would at a dismal treatise rouse and stir
As life were in't: I have supp'd full with horrors;
Direness, familiar to my slaughterous thoughts
Cannot once start me.

Re-enter SEYTON

Wherefore was that cry?

SEYTON

The queen, my lord, is dead.

MACBETH

She should have died hereafter;
There would have been a time for such a word.
To-morrow, and to-morrow, and to-morrow,
Creeps in this petty pace from day to day
To the last syllable of recorded time,
And all our yesterdays have lighted fools
The way to dusty death. Out, out, brief candle!
Life's but a walking shadow, a poor player
That struts and frets his hour upon the stage
And then is heard no more: it is a tale
Told by an idiot, full of sound and fury,
Signifying nothing.

Enter a Messenger

Thou comest to use thy tongue; thy story quickly.

Messenger

Gracious my lord,
I should report that which I say I saw,
But know not how to do it.

MACBETH

Well, say, sir.

Messenger

As I did stand my watch upon the hill,
I look'd toward Birnam, and anon, methought,
The wood began to move.

MACBETH

Liar and slave!

Messenger

Let me endure your wrath, if't be not so:
Within this three mile may you see it coming;
I say, a moving grove.

MACBETH

If thou speak'st false,
Upon the next tree shalt thou hang alive,

Till famine cling thee: if thy speech be sooth,
I care not if thou dost for me as much.
I pull in resolution, and begin
To doubt the equivocation of the fiend
That lies like truth: "Fear not, till Birnam Wood
Do come to Dunsinane:" and now a wood
Comes toward Dunsinane. Arm, arm, and out!
If this which he avouches does appear,
There is nor flying hence nor tarrying here.
I gin to be aweary of the sun,
And wish the estate o' the world were now undone.
Ring the alarum-bell! Blow, wind! come, wrack!
At least we'll die with harness on our back.

Exeunt

SCENE VI. Dunsinane. Before the Castle

Drum and colours. Enter MALCOLM, SIWARD, MACDUFF, and their Army, with boughs

MALCOLM

Now near enough: your leafy screens throw down.
And show like those you are. You, worthy uncle,
Shall, with my cousin, your right-noble son,
Lead our first battle: worthy Macduff and we
Shall take upon 's what else remains to do,
According to our order.

SIWARD

Fare you well.
Do we but find the tyrant's power to-night,
Let us be beaten, if we cannot fight.

MACDUFF

Make all our trumpets speak; give them all breath,
Those clamorous harbingers of blood and death.

Exeunt

SCENE VII. Another Part of the Field

Alarums. Enter MACBETH

MACBETH

They have tied me to a stake; I cannot fly,
But, bear-like, I must fight the course. What's he

That was not born of woman? Such a one
Am I to fear, or none.

Enter YOUNG SIWARD

YOUNG SIWARD

What is thy name?

MACBETH

Thou'lt be afraid to hear it.

YOUNG SIWARD

No; though thou call'st thyself a hotter name
Than any is in hell.

MACBETH

My name's Macbeth.

YOUNG SIWARD

The devil himself could not pronounce a title
More hateful to mine ear.

MACBETH

No, nor more fearful.

YOUNG SIWARD

Thou liest, abhorred tyrant; with my sword
I'll prove the lie thou speak'st.

They fight and YOUNG SIWARD is slain

MACBETH

Thou wast born of woman
But swords I smile at, weapons laugh to scorn,
Brandish'd by man that's of a woman born.

Exit

Alarums. Enter MACDUFF

MACDUFF

That way the noise is. Tyrant, show thy face!
If thou be'st slain and with no stroke of mine,
My wife and children's ghosts will haunt me still.
I cannot strike at wretched kerns, whose arms
Are hired to bear their staves: either thou, Macbeth,
Or else my sword with an unbatter'd edge

I sheathe again undeeded. There thou shouldst be;
By this great clatter, one of greatest note
Seems bruited. Let me find him, fortune!
And more I beg not.

Exit. Alarums

Enter MALCOLM and SIWARD

SIWARD

This way, my lord; the castle's gently render'd:
The tyrant's people on both sides do fight;
The noble thanes do bravely in the war;
The day almost itself professes yours,
And little is to do.

MALCOLM

We have met with foes
That strike beside us.

SIWARD

Enter, sir, the castle.

Exeunt. Alarums

SCENE VIII. Another Part of the Field

Enter MACBETH

MACBETH

Why should I play the Roman fool, and die
On mine own sword? whiles I see lives, the gashes
Do better upon them.
Enter MACDUFF

MACDUFF

Turn, hell-hound, turn!

MACBETH

Of all men else I have avoided thee:
But get thee back; my soul is too much charged
With blood of thine already.

MACDUFF

I have no words:
My voice is in my sword: thou bloodier villain
Than terms can give thee out!
They fight

MACBETH

Thou losest labour:
As easy mayst thou the intrenchant air
With thy keen sword impress as make me bleed:
Let fall thy blade on vulnerable crests;
I bear a charmed life, which must not yield,
To one of woman born.

MACDUFF

Despair thy charm;
And let the angel whom thou still hast served
Tell thee, Macduff was from his mother's womb
Untimely ripp'd.

MACBETH

Accursed be that tongue that tells me so,
For it hath cow'd my better part of man!
And be these juggling fiends no more believed,
That palter with us in a double sense;
That keep the word of promise to our ear,
And break it to our hope. I'll not fight with thee.

MACDUFF

Then yield thee, coward,
And live to be the show and gaze o' the time:
We'll have thee, as our rarer monsters are,
Painted on a pole, and underwrit,
'Here may you see the tyrant.'

MACBETH

I will not yield,
To kiss the ground before young Malcolm's feet,
And to be baited with the rabble's curse.
Though Birnam Wood be come to Dunsinane,
And thou opposed, being of no woman born,
Yet I will try the last. Before my body
I throw my warlike shield. Lay on, Macduff,
And damn'd be him that first cries, 'Hold, enough!'

Exeunt, fighting. Alarums

Retreat. Flourish. Enter, with drum and colours, MALCOLM, SIWARD, ROSS, the other Thanes, and Soldiers

MALCOLM

I would the friends we miss were safe arrived.

SIWARD

Some must go off: and yet, by these I see,
So great a day as this is cheaply bought.

MALCOLM

Macduff is missing, and your noble son.

ROSS

Your son, my lord, has paid a soldier's debt:
He only lived but till he was a man;
The which no sooner had his prowess confirm'd
In the unshrinking station where he fought,
But like a man he died.

SIWARD

Then he is dead?

ROSS

Ay, and brought off the field: your cause of sorrow
Must not be measured by his worth, for then
It hath no end.

SIWARD

Had he his hurts before?

ROSS

Ay, on the front.

SIWARD

Why then, God's soldier be he!
Had I as many sons as I have hairs,
I would not wish them to a fairer death:
And so, his knell is knoll'd.

MALCOLM

He's worth more sorrow,
And that I'll spend for him.

SIWARD

He's worth no more
They say he parted well, and paid his score:

And so, God be with him! Here comes newer comfort.
Re-enter MACDUFF, with MACBETH's head

MACDUFF

Hail, king! for so thou art: behold, where stands
The usurper's cursed head: the time is free:
I see thee compass'd with thy kingdom's pearl,
That speak my salutation in their minds;
Whose voices I desire aloud with mine:
Hail, King of Scotland!

ALL

Hail, King of Scotland!

Flourish

MALCOLM

We shall not spend a large expense of time
Before we reckon with your several loves,
And make us even with you. My thanes and kinsmen,
Henceforth be earls, the first that ever Scotland
In such an honour named. What's more to do,
Which would be planted newly with the time,
As calling home our exiled friends abroad
That fled the snares of watchful tyranny;
Producing forth the cruel ministers
Of this dead butcher and his fiend-like queen,
Who, as 'tis thought, by self and violent hands
Took off her life; this, and what needful else
That calls upon us, by the grace of Grace,
We will perform in measure, time and place:
So, thanks to all at once and to each one,
Whom we invite to see us crown'd at Scone.

Flourish. Exeunt

3

Summary with Critical Analysis

3.0 Objectives

After studying this unit you will be able:

- to understand the plot of the play *Macbeth*,
- to analyse each act,
- to study the political behavior of all the major characters in the play,
- to study psychological state of the characters,
- to mark the contemporary relevance of the play.

3.1 Introduction

In this unit, we learn the plot of the play and try to analyse each act properly. The play comprises five acts and each act has four to eight scenes in it. We will come to know that with the exception of Hamlet, the character of Macbeth is the most complex that Shakespeare has ever portrayed. It is complex in the sense that its motives cannot be analysed and labelled. Macbeth's imagination and sensibilities are better elements in his nature. His weakness of will is more responsible for his crime. It is usual to refer to Macbeth as a tragedy of ambition. With a certain justification, ambition does act as a determining passion in the play. It moves Macbeth and Lady Macbeth to the murder of King Duncan. The play is really a study in fear.

3.2 Act I

3.2.1 Act I, Scene I

Summary: The story of this play opens in ancient Scotland during a time of war. In thunder and lightning, near the place of battle, three witches meet on a lonely heath. They plan to meet again just before sunset, and speak to Macbeth as he returns victorious from the battlefield. Then they vanish into the storm.

Critical Analysis: Witches are the personifications of evil. The fog and filthy air suit the witches most. A reference to the central character of the play, Macbeth has been made in the opening scene. Thus, a relationship between the witches and Macbeth is shown in the very opening of the play. Witches are a symbol for the force of evil in the world. The witches offer a promise of worldly good.

3.2.2 Act I, Scene II

Summary: Duncan, the king of Scotland, waits for the news of the battle. A bleeding sergeant arrives to tell him of the valour of his general, Macbeth. The king also gets information about the treacherous behaviour of one of his noblemen, the Thane of Cawdor. The king is greatly impressed by the heroism displayed by Macbeth on the battlefield. The bleeding sergeant who comes from the battlefield informs King Duncan that Macbeth has shown great valour in the battlefield. He describes Macbeth as "Valour's minion." The sergeant also praises bravery of Banquo, another general who has fought side by side with Macbeth. Soon Ross and Angus, two noblemen appear with additional news of the battle. They tell the king that they have got victory mainly because of Macbeth whom they describe as "Bellona's bridegroom." The king orders the immediate execution of the treacherous Thane of Cawdor and decides to confer that title upon Macbeth.

Analysis: In this scene, Macbeth is depicted as hero. He is the general of great valour and heroic spirit. The sergeant and soon afterwards Ross and Angus describe qualities of Macbeth. The title of Thane of Cawdor is conferred upon Macbeth. The Thane of Cawdor proved a traitor. Macbeth too will prove soon. There is the dramatic irony in the remark of Duncan: "What he hath lost, noble Macbeth hath won."

3.2.3 Act I, Scene III

Summary: The three witches meet again, as they had already arranged a gathering. They discuss about what they have been doing. Their discussion shows that they are malicious and revengeful. First witch discloses her plan to torture a sailor whose wife has insulted her. All three sing together a spell to wind up the charm.

While returning from the battlefield, Macbeth and Banquo are greeted by the three witches. The first witch says: "All hail, Macbeth! Hail to thee, Thane of Glamis!" The second witch says: "All hail, Macbeth! Hail to thee, Thane of Cawdor!" The third witch says: "All hail, Macbeth that shalt be king hereafter!" Macbeth feels too upset to answer. After listening to his companion's future, Banquo asks them about his future. The three witches greet Banquo one after the other. The first witch says that Banquo's status is lower than that of Macbeth yet higher. The second witch tells him that he is not as fortunate as Macbeth, and yet in a sense more fortunate than him. The third witch predicts that he will never be a king, but his descendents will be kings. Then the witches disappear.

After sometime, Ross and Angus, the noblemen welcome Macbeth and Banquo. Ross informs Macbeth that King Duncan has conferred upon him the title of the Thane of Cawdor who has been sentenced to death for his disloyalty. This information indicates the partial fulfillment of the prophecy of the witches. In an aside, Macbeth imagines himself attaining the position of the King of Scotland but only through an awful deed. The thought of ambition makes him agitated.

Analysis: The witches possess supernatural power and their character is evil. There is the mysterious link between Macbeth and the three witches. Macbeth's remark: "So foul and fair a day I have not seen before" is an echo of the witches statement that "Fair is foul, and foul is fair." The prophesies of the witches determine the entire plot of the play. In an aside, Macbeth reveals his secret thoughts. However, he is able to remove the evil thought from his mind quickly and says that fortune may take its own course.

3.2.4 Act I, Scene IV

Summary: Macbeth and Banquo arrive in the palace to meet King Duncan. King Duncan expresses deep gratitude towards both generals who have rendered great service to the nation.

Duncan then proceeds to announce the nomination of his eldest son, Malcolm, as the heir to the throne. This announcement comes as a big blow to Macbeth. Macbeth thinks that the nomination of heir is an obstacle in the way of his becoming the King of Scotland. He considers that the assassination of King Duncan is the only way open for him to become the King of Scotland. Duncan's comment on the Thane of Cawdor, who has been executed, is significant. Duncan says that there is no art by which one can know the secret working of another's mind. There is the dramatic irony in the comment because the view is applicable to Macbeth also.

Analysis: King Duncan is a simple minded and trustful king. He expresses gratitude towards those who have served him well. He would like to visit Macbeth's castle at Inverness in order to appreciate his great deeds in the wartime situation. Macbeth's aside shows the working of his mind. Previously, he suppressed evil thoughts which arose in his mind. Now he asks stars to extinguish their light so that his dark and black desires are not exposed. The thought of assassinating King Duncan becomes stronger in his mind.

3.2.5 Act I, Scene V

Summary: Lady Macbeth reads the letter written to her by her husband after his meeting with the witches. After reading the contents of the letter Lady Macbeth thinks that the crown of Scotland is waiting for her husband. She believes that her husband's kind nature is an obstacle to get the throne. She knows that her husband is "too full of the milk of human kindness."

A messenger comes and informs Lady Macbeth that the King of Scotland, Duncan is coming to her castle that very night as a guest. Lady Macbeth considers that this visit is a good opportunity for her husband to kill Duncan. In a soliloquy, she appeals to the forces of evil to crush all feminine weakness in her and fill her with the utmost cruelty so that she may not spare the life of Duncan.

When Macbeth arrives, Lady Macbeth greets him with the words, with which the witches had greeted him. She asks him to be prepared to murder Duncan. She asks him to look like the innocent flower but be the serpent under it. Macbeth replies that they will speak further about it. Lady Macbeth is determined. Macbeth is not resolute about the evil action.

Analysis: This scene makes us aware about the natures of both Macbeth and Lady Macbeth. The two great soliloquies reveal her character. She thinks that her husband is not wicked to kill Duncan. She also believes that her husband is ambitious but he is not wicked to follow the shortest way to get crown. She instigates him to perform the evil action.

Her soliloquies reveal Lady Macbeth as a woman of strong determination and hard heart. She is cunning and hypocritical. She asks the evil forces to expel the milk in her breast and fill it with poison. She allows nothing to come between her determination and its realization. She is firm and determined.

3.2.6 Act I, Scene VI

Summary: King Duncan arrives at Inverness in the company of his sons, Malcolm and Donalbain, and a few of his noblemen, Banquo, Lenox, Macduff, Ross, and Angus. He thinks the atmosphere of the castle, is very pleasant and wholesome. He is welcomed by Lady Macbeth with the expression of joy. Lady Macbeth expresses her loyalty and devotion to him.

Analysis: This scene is ironic. Duncan admires the atmosphere of the castle. Banquo too is full of praise for the bright atmosphere of the castle. Lady Macbeth expresses fidelity and loyalty to the guest. Inwardly, she has the quite opposite feeling of disloyalty. King Duncan does not realize what danger is awaiting him at that pleasant castle. This is the scene which can be called as an example of dramatic irony.

3.2.7 Act I, Scene VII

Summary: This scene introduces us to the working of Macbeth's mind. Macbeth thinks of the difficulties in the way of murdering King. He thinks of the horrible consequences of evil action. King Duncan has been a fair and modest king. He is his relative, monarch, and guest. He knows his duty is to protect the king rather than himself playing the murderer. He says that because of his inordinate ambition, he will not commit a horrible crime. He tells his wife that he will proceed no further in this business.

Lady Macbeth instigates her husband to kill the king. She assures him that the task will not fail. She had already thought of a plan that suspicion will fall upon the two guards who will be on duty outside King Duncan's bed chamber. Macbeth cannot resist the strong urgings of his wife. Macbeth resolves to murder the king under his wife's strong instigation.

Analysis: This scene introduces us to Macbeth's state of mind when he is contemplating the murder of King Duncan. Macbeth feels afraid of the horrible consequences of the crime of assassinating the king. He also realizes the fact that a person, who prepares a cup of poison for another, is generally compelled to drink it himself. He also thinks about the excellent qualities which King Duncan possesses. He tells to his wife that they will not proceed in this business.

Lady Macbeth instigates her husband to commit the crime. She is ruthless. Once resolved she does not waver. If Lady Macbeth does not instigate him constantly, her husband might have given up the plan to murder King Duncan to get the monarchy of Scotland. Lady Macbeth mocks her husband that he lacks the courage. This is a taunt which a general cannot bear. She asks him that he should not waver in the enterprise. In her speech, she tells that she could have dashed out the brains of a baby to murder Duncan if once she resolved. This shows her ruthlessness.

3.3 Act II

3.3.1 Act II, Scene I

Duncan arrives at the castle of Macbeth. Banquo feels too restless to sleep. Certain cursed thoughts make him restless. In the courtyard, he encounters Macbeth. Both of them are restless. Banquo discusses with Macbeth about the three witches. Macbeth tells him that he is not thinking of them. Macbeth then asks Banquo to support and stand by him in the time of need. Banquo assures him that certainly he will do so, provided he does not deviate himself from the path of truth and honesty.

Macbeth now waits for the signal from his wife. The signal is the indication that the guards are drunk and fast asleep. While waiting, his imagination begins to work, he sees a visionary dagger before him. He tries to seize the dagger but cannot do so. The dagger exists only in the imagination. It is not a real dagger. He sees that the dagger is moving towards Duncan's bed chamber. His bloody intention has created the image of dagger. He now thinks of witches, wolves, rape and murder, the things related with the darkness and night.

Analysis: This scene reveals us the character of Banquo. Banquo also somewhat has been affected by the weird sisters' prophecy as he dreamt of them last night. He also tells to Macbeth during their conversation that he will never deviate from the path of virtue.

In the soliloquy, we come to know about the thoughts in the mind of Macbeth. He talks to dagger, which his guilty mind has created. He also thinks of the different types of crimes committed in the darkness of the night. Macbeth himself is to use a dagger to kill King Duncan. His guilty mind has created an image of a dagger. The imaginary dagger corresponds to the real dagger. This scene leads to the assassination of King Duncan which is the central incident of the play.

3.3.2 Act II, Scene II

Summary: In the soliloquy, Lady Macbeth tells that she drugged the guards to sleep. She put a drug in their drink. She says that if Duncan had not resembled her father, she would have killed him herself.

Macbeth appears and tells his wife that he has assassinated the king and whether she heard a noise. He tells her that as he descended the stairs someone said prayers, Macbeth had tried to say "Amen" but he had not been able to utter the word "Amen." He thinks over his inability to say the word "Amen." Lady Macbeth asks him not to think over the matters; otherwise they will drive them mad. He thinks someone cried to him, "Sleep no more." He thinks he will never again be able to enjoy the innocent sleep, sleep which is the chief sustainer of life. He thinks that he had murdered the sleep, by committing the horrible crime of murder. Lady Macbeth asks her husband to get some water and wash the stains of blood from his hand, for stains are the witness of his crime. She asks him to take back the dagger he has brought with him and put it back in the hands of attendants and smear them with blood, so that suspicion will fall upon them. Macbeth feels guilty. He thinks that all the oceans of the world cannot clean the stains of blood from his hand. On the other hand, the stains on his hand will turn the green water into red. Lady Macbeth smears the guards with blood. Now her own hands are also red. She thinks that "A little water clears us of this deed." She hears knocking at the South gate. There is more knocking. Macbeth expresses the desire that knocking would wake Duncan that is to bring him back to life.

Analysis: This scene depicts the climax of the first movement of the play. The main incident, the assassination of King Duncan takes place in this scene. This scene is also important from the psychological perspective. Lady Macbeth possesses the essential feminity. She is a woman of strong resolution. She gives extravagant speech. She drinks wine to acquire necessary courage to face the situation. She cannot herself assassinate the king, because Duncan seemed to resemble her father.

In this scene, we also come to know about the guilty conscience of Macbeth. He realizes now the evil consequences of the horrible crime.

3.3.3 Act II, Scene III

Summary: The gatekeeper at the gate of the castle, hears the knocking at the gate, but is drunk, sleepy and slow to answer. In a comic soliloquy, the gatekeeper thinks if a man were a porter at the gate of hell, how hard he would have to work. He gets amused for a little while by imagining that he is really the porter at the gate of hell. He opens the gate and admits Macduff and Lenox who have come to awaken the king at the hour which had been fixed by the king. Macbeth now receives the two noblemen. While Macduff goes to rouse the king, Lenox speaks to Macbeth of the terrible storm that had been blowing during the night and the earthquakes which had shaken the earth. Macbeth replies that it really was a violent night. Macduff now returns crying "O horror! Horror! Horror!" What has happened is beyond the tongue to speak and hard to imagine. Macduff tells that the king has been murdered. The whole castle is now thrown into havoc.

Macbeth quickly kills the two guards ostensibly because they have obviously committed the murder. Macbeth was afraid that guards should plead their innocence, and thus create a complication for him. He justifies killing the guards on the plea that he could not endure to have such treacherous murderers alive. Macbeth and Lady Macbeth both play their part very well at this moment.

Macbeth expresses a feeling of profound sorrow over the assassination of King Duncan. He also says that the world has become empty and life has become futile with the death of their king.

Malcolm and Donalbain, the two sons of the murdered king believe that Macbeth has done the treachery. They think that their own lives are in danger. Malcolm says that it is very easy for a traitor to pretend the sorrow utterly unfelt by him. Donalbain says that "There's a dagger in men's smiles." Where they are there is treachery even in the smiles of men. The two brothers decide to leave Scotland for saving their lives. They mount on horses and ride away.

Critical Analysis: Some critics have said that the scene of porter's soliloquy is ironic. Because the scene resembles the porter at the gate of the hell in Mystery plays. Some critics believe that to give some type of essential comic relief at this point in the play, the comic scene is introduced.

The turmoil in nature corresponds to the murder of a great man. The owl, the bird of darkness shriek the whole night. The night has been unruly. The cries of the dead are heard in the air. The last night was very stormy. Some people say that the earth shook as if it were suffering from some fever. There are convulsions in nature as there are convulsions in human life. Macbeth shows a rare presence of mind in this scene. He kills the guards and defends his action by saying that how he could tolerate murderers of Duncan living a peaceful life. His self-assurance and self-possession does not last long. He says that Duncan's death is a great loss to the world. His speech is hypocritical. Lady Macbeth faints, it seems genuine. Malcolm and Donalbain think that their life is in danger; they take the decision to leave Scotland. Malcolm goes to England. Donalbain goes to Ireland.

3.3.4 Act II, Scene IV

Summary: Ross talks to an old man outside the castle of Inverness. The old man is seventy years old. He has been a witness to strange events and happenings. The old man says that during the whole of his life, he does not remember having witnessed such a dreadful night. Ross agrees and expresses his own feelings on the occasion. He says that although now it is day time, the sun seems to have been strangled by darkness. The old man says that this darkness during the time is as unnatural as the murder of the king that was committed during the night.

Macduff informs Ross that Malcolm and Donalbain have fled from Inverness and from Scotland. The two sons of the king have secretly run away. The suspicion of the king's murder therefore has fallen upon them. Macduff also reveals that Macbeth soon will be crowned as the king. He has gone to Scone to be crowned.

Critical Analysis: Some supernatural portents and prodigies precede Duncan's murder. A falcon, flying at its full pitch, is attacked and killed by an owl which generally flies low and hunts only mice. Duncan's horses have broken out of their stalls, defied their keepers, and devoured each other. These portents strengthen our impression that Nature sympathizes with human beings. The assassination of the king is preceded by events in the world of nature which are a complete deviation from normal. Macbeth's ambition is now fulfilled. He is crowned as the king. Another part of the witches' prophecy comes true.

3.4 Act III

3.4.1 Act III, Scene I

This scene begins with a soliloquy by Banquo. He thinks that all the prophecies of the witches, related to Macbeth, have been fulfilled. He ponders that as the prophecies related to Macbeth have already proved true, their prophecies related to him also will come true.

Macbeth now has become King of Scotland. Lady Macbeth has now become the Queen. The King and the Queen hold a state banquet at night. Most of the noblemen including Banquo have been invited. Macbeth requests Banquo to attend the banquet. He will be the chief guest at the banquet. Banquo assures Macbeth that he will attend the banquet. Banquo, at this moment is about to ride away on some business in the company of his son, Fleance, he promises Macbeth that he and his son will come back by the time at which the banquet is to be held.

Macbeth then sends away all his noblemen and attendants, as he wishes to be alone till the time of the banquet. In a soliloquy, he expresses the apprehension that his fears of Banquo are deep rooted. He says that Banquo possesses such royal dignity as would inspire awe in anyone. He is a man of great daring. His wisdom guides him in all that he undertakes to do. There is no one except Banquo whom he fears. The witches' prophecy about Banquo troubles him most. The weird sisters had said that Banquo's descendents will be the kings; Macbeth's descendents will not be the kings. He thinks that he despoiled his mind for the benefit of Banquo's children. He has murdered the gracious King Duncan. He has poisoned the peace of his own mind. It appears that the entire he has done ultimately is for the benefit to Banquo's children. Macbeth has therefore been thinking of killing Banquo and his son.

Two murderers come to meet Macbeth. Macbeth tells them that Banquo had done injustice to them. He also tells them that Banquo has ruined them. He urges them to take revenge upon him. The two murderers promise Macbeth that they will carry out, Macbeth's command; they will kill both Banquo and Fleance.

Critical Analysis: Banquo harbours an ambition. Banquo's soliloquy in this scene shows that he is also affected by the prophecy of the witches. He secretly harbours the thought that his descendents might after all rule over Scotland. He is also partly ambitious. He would be happy if he becomes the founder of a dynasty.

Macbeth has now become a seasoned intriguer. He diplomatically obtains the information from Banquo about his movements during the day, so that he can pass on this information to the two murderers. His conversation with the two murderers shows that he has become proficient in working upon other people's grievances and using those people for his own purpose. He explains to them that they have some common friends;

otherwise he would have killed him openly. He values goodwill and friendship of common friends. He also asks them to keep it a secret. He entrusted the murderers to kill both Banquo, and his son, Fleance, in the darkness of the night. Now, Macbeth is not the simple person, we met in the beginning of the play.

In the soliloquy, Macbeth accepts his moral inferiority to Banquo. He says that in presence of Banquo his better nature is rebuked, just as Antony felt his better nature rebuked in presence of Caesar. This scene also builds up an atmosphere of suspense. Now it is very interesting to see what course the plot to kill Banquo and Fleance would take. Macbeth commissioned the murderers to kill.

3.4.2 Act III, Scene II

Summary: Lady Macbeth in a short soliloquy expresses the feeling that they have attained their goal of monarchy, but lost the peace of mind. Her desire to see her husband as the King of Scotland has been fulfilled, but she has lost the peace of mind. Lady Macbeth asks her husband why he is keeping himself alone. She tells him that things without remedies should not be thought of at all. Lady Macbeth tells him to compose his troubled looks. He should be cheerful as he moves among his guests at night. Macbeth says that his mind is full of scorpions, and will remain so as long as Banquo and Fleance are alive. He does not tell to his wife complete details of the conspiracy.

Critical Analysis: This scene is very important from psychological point of view. It is important because the states of the minds of the two major characters, who are responsible for the crime of assassination of their king, have been portrayed effectively. Both Macbeth and Lady Macbeth feel mental torture. They have lost the peace of mind, because they have killed a gracious and rightful king. Lady Macbeth tries to overcome her mental suffering. She offers consolation and comfort to her husband. Macbeth tells her that he suffers mental anguish because of crime. He does not reveal to her the plot which he has hatched for the murder of Banquo and Fleance. His withholding this secret from Lady Macbeth is a sign that he is drifting away from her.

Macbeth is a man of poetic nature. He possesses an exceptional ability to express his thoughts in language that is powerful and vivid. His imaginative power and his power of expression are commendable. Indeed, he has the soul of a poet. His feeling of ambition has forced him to follow the path of evil.

3.4.3 Act III, Scene III

Summary: This scene describes that the two murderers are lying in ambush for Banquo and Fleance. They are joined by a third murderer with whom they were not previously acquainted. He tells them that he has been sent by Macbeth to assist them. As soon as Banquo and Fleance arrive and dismount from their horses, the Murderers attack them. Banquo is killed, and Fleance manages to escape. Thus, only half of the task assigned to the three murderers has been executed.

Critical Analysis: This is a melodramatic scene. It has sensational effect on our minds. It is a very thrilling and tragic scene. An innocent man Banquo is killed. Macbeth has now become a tyrant. A good person now seems to him a source of danger. So he killed him. Macbeth has taken extra precaution for his conspiracy against Banquo. He has sent the third murderer to make it sure that the other two do not betray him, and also to provide them an additional helper. Macbeth has now become an accomplished conspirator.

3.4.4 Act III, Scene IV

Summary: The state banquet is ready. Macbeth, Lady Macbeth, and the noblemen arrive for the great occasion. Macbeth begins to mingle with the guests to speak word of welcome to them. Suddenly, he sees one of the murderers at the gate and goes quickly to meet him. The murderer tells him that Banquo has been killed but Fleance has escaped. Fleance's escape comes as a great blow to Macbeth's plans. He sends away the murderer and rejoins the feast.

Macbeth, when tries to occupy the seat meant for him, he views Banquo's ghost sitting in the chair. He is frightened. He addresses the ghost. He tells to the ghost that he cannot say that he has done it. The guests are surprised to see Macbeth talking to an empty chair, because the ghost is not visible to anyone else.

Lady Macbeth at once understands the situation that her husband has seen the hallucination. She tries her utmost to awaken him to the reality and enable him to get rid of his fear. She tells to the guests that her husband has often been subject to such fit even from his youth. She tells them that fit will soon be over. Macbeth talks to the ghost till it disappears.

Macbeth expresses his surprise that a dead man has risen and come to confront him. Lady Macbeth explains to the guests so that the guests should not suspect the truth. She tells them that this strange behaviour is quite usual with him. Macbeth apologizes to the guests that he suffers from a certain infirmity which is well known to those who are close to him. Macbeth orders for wine and that he would drink to everybody's health and happiness.

The ghost of Banquo reappears again in the banquet. Macbeth tells the ghost now to quit and not to bother him. He challenges the ghost. He asks the ghost to come in the shape of a man or a beast but not in the present shape to fight with him. The ghost disappears, and now Macbeth recovers his balance of mind. Macbeth asks if such things do really exist. He feels sorry that he felt frightened at this strange sight. Ross asks him what sight he is talking about. Lady Macbeth intervenes and tells Ross that Macbeth should not be cross examined. She bids a hasty good night to the guests, and requests them to leave her husband alone.

When the guests have gone, Macbeth tells his wife that the ghost had probably come to take revenge. He says, "It will have blood: they say blood will have blood." Stones move, and trees speak to reveal murders. Any murder does not remain a mystery. Birds, rooks, maggot-pies, and crows have known to reveal the murders kept as a great secret. Macbeth now talks about the next danger he faces. He tells Lady Macbeth that Macduff seems to be hostile to him; he would like to do something to suppress that man. Macduff refuses to present himself in spite of his specific orders. He refuses to come. Macbeth says that he will go to the Weird Sisters the very next day to know more about his future. Compared with his own good, all other considerations are secondary. He says that he is so far advanced in this bloody deed that it is now a difficult to retreat as to go ahead. He tells that he is now novice in crime but soon he will become hardened.

Critical Analysis: This scene is very effective due to supernatural elements which create an atmosphere of mystery, suspense, and horror. Macbeth is the only person who saw Banquo's ghost at the banquet. Lady Macbeth or even any other nobleman did not see the ghost. The ghost is a subjective apparition. The ghost is a personification of Macbeth's sense of guilt. His conscience torments him for the murder of Banquo. He has yet not become a confirmed butcher. He is on the way to become one. Previously, he had seen an imaginary dagger, now he sees the ghost. These are the results of his guilty conscience.

Lady Macbeth plays a very important role in this scene. As soon as Lady Macbeth knows that her husband has succumbed to fears, he has the hallucination of ghost; she takes the control of the situation. She encourages him to restore to normalcy. She also explains to the guests that these fits are periodically usual with him. Lady Macbeth has a presence of mind; she also shows her quality of leadership. She has saved the situation. Macbeth might have betrayed himself.

3.4.5 Act III, Scene V

Summary: Hecate, the goddess of witchcraft, gives some instructions to the three witches. She rebukes them for having not informed of what they have been doing to Macbeth. They had never invited her to play her part in the matter of doing evil to others. Hecate asks them to amend their previous negligence. She also informs them that Macbeth is coming to them to know his future. She tells them to be ready with their charms and spells. As for herself, she would raise certain artificial spirits who will work for the ruin of this man. By the force of illusion, Macbeth will be enticed to his own destruction.

Critical Analysis: In this scene, we meet the three witches again. They receive some instructions from Hecate about how they should deal with Macbeth. This is a supernatural scene. It creates feelings of suspense, mystery, and terror. The supernatural powers here are all totally evil.

3.4.6 Act III, Scene VI

Summary: Two Scottish noblemen discuss the situation in Scotland. Lenox discusses the situation with another nobleman. Lenox comments adversely on the actions of Macbeth. He indirectly accuses Macbeth for the murder of King Duncan and Banquo. Lenox also says that the two sons of King Duncan, Malcolm, and Donalbain, would also have been in great danger, if they had not fled from Scotland. Likewise, Fleance would have been killed if he had not managed to escape. According to Lenox, now Macduff has incurred the wrath of Macbeth and lives in disgrace. He says that so far Macbeth has managed everything very cleverly. Macduff talks plainly about the situation in his country. He refuses to attend the banquet given by this tyrant. Therefore, he has already incurred his displeasure. The other nobleman informs Lenox that Malcolm has been kindly received by the saintly King Edward. Malcolm hopes to get support of the King Edward to fight against Macbeth in order to attain the Scottish crown to which he is legally entitled.

Critical Analysis: Certain future developments are suggested in this scene. The Scottish noblemen have now become aware about the criminal who murdered King Duncan. The future course of events is hinted at through the report that Malcolm hopes to get the support of King of England to fight against Macbeth. Macduff now lives in disgrace; this information also suggests certain future events.

The long speech that Lenox makes at the beginning of the scene is full of irony. Lenox speaks ironically about the murders that have been committed. His intention is to convey the meaning indirectly to the Lord rather than in plain terms. His use of ironic language to convey the facts show the atmosphere of terror that prevailed in Scotland. The noblemen in Scotland cannot dare to oppose Macbeth, though they have become aware about the truth about the murders.

3.5 Act IV

3.5.1 Act IV, Scene I

Summary: The witches are once again introduced here. They prepare a magic broth from strange ingredients. They prepare the strong broth for the devil. They boil and bake in the cauldron the pieces of a snake caught in a fen, the eye of a newt, the toe of a frog, the hair of a bat, the tongue of a dog, the forked tongue of a snake, the sting of a glow-worm, the leg of a lizard, and a wing of an owl. As the witches watch the cauldron boiling, they all sing their incantation which indicates that their object is to multiply the toil and trouble which human beings have to suffer in this world. They go round the cauldron singing and dancing like elves and fairies in a ring uttering the magic spell on the things they are putting in the cauldron. Hecate arrives and compliments them for well done broth. One of the witches informs the other that the pricking sensation in her thumb suggests that someone wicked is coming to meet them.

The wicked person who arrives is no other than Macbeth. He calls upon the witches to answer his questions, and provide him the information he needs, even in giving such information they have to bring about great ruin and destruction in the world. The witches know what questions Macbeth wants to ask them. A number of apparitions come before Macbeth to give the information he needs about future. The first apparition is an armed head which tells Macbeth that he should beware of Macduff, the Thane of Fife. The second apparition is a bloody child who tells Macbeth to be bloody, bold and determined, to resist the power of man, because he can never be harmed by anyone born of a woman. The third apparition is a crowned child holding a tree in its hand. This apparition suggests that Macbeth will never be defeated in battle till Birnam Wood moves to Dusinane to fight against him.

Macbeth is not satisfied with the information so far he has received from the Weird Sisters. He welcomes whatever information he has got from them. The witches then show him eight kings followed by Banquo who holds a mirror in his hand, and is smiling at Macbeth. Macbeth comes to know that eight kings represent Banquo's descendents who will rule over Scotland.

The witches then disappear. Lenox comes to meet Macbeth with the news that Macduff has fled to England. After hearing the news, Macbeth gives order to seize Macduff's castle. He also gives order to kill his wife and children.

Critical Analysis: The supernatural scene here creates an atmosphere of mystery and terror. The witches tell information to Macbeth about his future, but some of the facts he already knows. He already knows that Macduff represents danger. Previously, the witches had told him that Banquo's descendents will rule over Scotland. However, two new facts are revealed to Macbeth that he need not fear any man born of a woman, and he cannot be defeated until Birnam Wood moves to Dunsinane to fight against him. These two prophecies create in Macbeth a feeling of complete security. This was Hecate's intention. Because she had told the three witches: "Security is mortal's chiefest enemy."

In this scene, we notice a new development in Macbeth's character. He is now completely dominated by a lust for power. He has discarded his moral sense of right and wrong which was very strong in his mind at one time. He does not care if witches do a lot of destruction for telling him information about his future. The witches warn him to be aware of Macduff, he determines to kill Macduff. As soon as Lenox tells him that Macduff has fled to England, Macbeth orders to seize his castle and kill his wife and children.

3.5.2 Act IV, Scene II

Summary: Ross arrives in Macduff's castle and informs his wife that her husband has fled from Scotland. Lady Macduff tells that her husband's flight is an act of madness. Lady Macduff tells that her husband has not done anything for the protection of his family in his absence. She thinks that her husband lacks love for the family; therefore, he has not taken proper care of his family. Ross leaves the place. Lady Macduff tells her son that he should regard his father as being dead. The son asks his mother many questions. The mother tries to satisfy his curiosity.

A messenger now arrives and informs Lady Macduff that some danger is about to befall the family. He advises Lady Macduff to leave her castle at once along with the little ones. The messenger goes away and Lady Macduff wonders where she should go. She knows that she has done no harm to anyone in the world. She understands that in this wicked world, doing harm is accepted as commendable and doing well is sometimes thought to be a dangerous folly. A number of ruffians arrive. One of them stabs Macduff's son who cries to his mother to run away, but the ruffians pursue Lady Macduff in order to kill her.

Critical Analysis: Macduff has behaved in an irresponsible manner towards his family. He left Scotland without doing any security arrangement for his family. He cannot justify his action. He lacks a sense of duty towards his wife and children. His patriotism and integrity cannot get rid of our impression of his negligent behaviour towards his family.

This scene shows the atmosphere of fear and horror. The ruffians arrive and kill Lady Macduff and her son. Our hearts are full of pity for the innocent members of Macduff's family who died, even though they have done no harm to anyone.

We come to know in this scene that Macbeth has now become a ruthless tyrant. He ordered the ruffians to kill the innocent Lady Macduff and her son. This action shows that he has now become a hardened dictator and is ready to go to any length to secure his position. Till now, Macduff opposed Macbeth on political grounds, but now there develops personal enmity between them because of Macbeth's act of killing of his family. Eventually, it is Macduff who kills Macbeth.

3.5.3 Act IV, Scene III

Summary: Malcolm and Macduff, both of them are now in England; they are talking to each other about their misfortunes and about the wretched conditions prevailed in their country. Macduff tells to Malcolm about the terrible condition prevailed in Scotland. He describes the situation that every morning more and more women are turned into widows who bewail their loss; more children are made orphans who lament at their sorrow. Malcolm thinks that Macduff has come to him not as a supporter or ally but as a spy. Malcolm subjects Macduff to a hard test to determine whether he is loyal to him or to Macbeth. Macduff does not of course realize that he is being subjected to a test.

Malcolm pretends that he is a wicked man. When Macduff tries to arouse Malcolm's anger against Macbeth by telling that Malcolm is the rightful heir to the Scottish throne, Malcolm pretends not to be interested in Monarchy. Malcolm tells him that he lacks all those qualities which a man needs in order to function successfully as a king. He tells that he does not possess qualities befitting a king like, justice, truthfulness, self-restraint, firmness, generosity, perseverance, compassion, humility, devotion, patience, courage, and endurance. He says that if he had the power he would banish the sweet milk of peace and harmony from this earth into hell and bring about universal chaos and disorder.

Malcolm describes himself in such dark colours in order to know Macduff's sincerity. After listening self portrayal from Malcolm, Macduff tells that such person is not fit to rule over a nation, he is even not fit to live. After being convinced that Macduff is not a spy or an ally of Macbeth, Malcolm explains to him why he has described himself in dark colours. He assures Macduff that he does not suffer from the defects of character which he enumerated. He tells that he is yet unknown to love. He has not coveted even the things that are his own. Truth is dear to him as his own life. Macduff feels happy to listen to this true portrayal of Malcolm.

A doctor appears and tells Malcolm that the King of England, Edward, the Confessor, is coming soon to have an interview with him. At present the king is busy treating the patients who are suffering from incurable diseases. He has the remarkable power of curing patients; he also possesses the power of prophecy.

Ross now arrives and informs Malcolm that Scotland is passing through a period of great suffering and agony. Their country cannot be called mother but grave. In Scotland, now the air is full of sighs, groans, shrieks. Men either are dying or they are killed.

Ross then reveals to Macduff the massacre of Macduff's family. Macduff's wife and children are cruelly killed by the ruffians sent by Macbeth. Macduff's grief knows no bounds. He prays to God to give him an opportunity to take revenge upon the ruthless dictator, Macbeth. Malcolm tells to Macduff that time has come to take the revenge. Forces of the English King are ready. Malcolm tells Macduff that they will invade Scotland and liberate it from the tyrannical clutches of the dictator, Macbeth.

Critical Analysis: In this scene, we come to know about the character of Malcolm. Shakespeare perhaps suggested through this scene that a king must possess certain important virtues to govern the country in an effective and good manner. Malcolm is virtuous and cautious person. He tests Macduff's loyalty through his conversation.

Macbeth has now become a ruthless dictator. The country suffers great misfortunes under his reign. Macbeth has become utterly reckless and desperate because of his feeling of fear.

Macbeth is quite opposite to the English king. The English King, Edward possesses certain beneficent qualities. He has the divine power to heal the people of incurable diseases. He has the ability to foresee the future. Macbeth has become obsessed with the feelings of ambition and fear. Now we do not feel any sympathy for Macbeth.

Macduff is a great patriot. He leaves Scotland to seek help from outside to free his country from tyranny. When he listens to the news that Macbeth has killed his complete family by sending murderers, he becomes furious. He now has developed a personal grudge against him. In due course, Macduff serves as the agent of divine retribution against Macbeth.

The final speech by Malcolm in this scene shows the beginning of the end of Macbeth's tyrannical monarchy. The tide has turned against him. He said that it is the time that Macbeth must be punished. Heavenly powers have now sent the instruments of vengeance.

3.6 Act V

3.6.1 Act V, Scene I

Summary: In this scene, we come to know that Lady Macbeth is mentally disturbed. She has been walking in her sleep during the night. A Waiting-Gentlewoman and a Doctor watch Lady Macbeth in her sleepwalking, hiding themselves. Lady Macbeth, during the course of her sleepwalking, talks to herself about the assassination of King Duncan, murder of Banquo, massacre of Macduff's wife and children. Doctor says, "Unnatural deeds do breed unnatural troubles." The Doctor advises the Waiting-

Gentlewoman, to take care of Lady Macbeth. He also tells her to keep watch upon her, keep away from her anything that she might use to bring harm to herself.

Critical Analysis: In this scene, Lady Macbeth shows her essential feminity. Lady Macbeth is after all a woman of sensibility. The crimes of murder have moved her deeply. She has lost her peace of mind. She is afraid of darkness. Her conscience torments her. Earlier she had said that a little water would clear her and her husband of the deed of murder. Now she repents the action of murder and says, "Here's the smell of the blood still: all the perfumes of Arabia will not sweeten this little hand. Oh! Oh! Oh!"

This scene shows that Lady Macbeth has lost her balance of mind. It shows that the evil action is self-destructive.

3.6.2 Act V, Scene II

Summary: This scene informs us that some of the Scottish nobles have revolted against Macbeth. The Scottish nobles, Menteith, Caithness, Angus, and Lenox have decided to support the English invading forces led by Malcolm. Caithness informs the other noblemen that Macbeth is fortifying the castle at Dunsinane. Some people report that he has gone mad. Macbeth has now become so wild in ambition that he has become out of control. Now the murders Macbeth committed secretly are haunting and tormenting him. Every minute there are some soldiers who revolt against him. Those soldiers who are still in his command are not because of any devotion for him, but because of military discipline. Caithness says that they must continue their march to offer their support to Malcolm who is coming to free Scotland from the tyranny of Macbeth.

Critical Analysis: This scene provides us the very important development in the plot of the play. It informs us that most of the Scottish nobles have left Macbeth. They and their soldiers are marching towards Birnam Wood where they will join the forces led by Malcolm. We also get the information that old Siward is one of the generals assisting Malcolm in his command of the English army. Young Siward is also coming to fight as a soldier in the English army. A hint is given that Macbeth will face the doom. Macbeth's soldiers obey him not because of feeling of love, but because of military discipline.

3.6.3 Act V, Scene III

Summary: Macbeth is in the fort at Dunsinane. He feels confident because of the Weird Sister's prophecy that no man born of woman can do any harm; he cannot be defeated till Birnam Wood moves to Dunsinane. However, a servant brings the news that ten thousand English soldiers have been sighted marching onwards to Dunsinane. Macbeth loses his temper. He rebukes the servant and calls him a coward.

Macbeth shows confidence outwardly. At heart he is disillusioned. He tells to Seyton that the present crisis will either strengthen his position for ever or will dethrone him. He compares his life to a dry yellow leaf in autumn. He expresses the sorrow that he will never enjoy honour, love, obedience, friends in great numbers.

A Doctor brings the news that Lady Macbeth's condition is worsening. Doctor tells that she is troubled with morbid fancies crowding into her mind and denies her rest and sleep. Macbeth urges the Doctor to cure her of her morbid fancies, burden of sadness which weighs upon her heart. Doctor replies that for this cure patient has to be responsive for the treatment. Macbeth feels irritated by the Doctor's reply. He gets ready for the approaching battle, though he too is not feeling healthy.

Critical Analysis: This scene reveals us the state of mind of Macbeth. In his mind, the feelings are mixed, he feels confident and he also feels sad. He feels confident only because of the witches' prophecy. His comparison of his life to a yellow leaf in autumn shows his despair and restlessness. Another important thing noticed is that he lacks feeling of deep attachment for his wife. He asks the Doctor to cure her of the disease but there is no deep feeling of love in his dialogue. What feeling has dominated him most is the fear of the approaching English army.

3.6.4 Act V, Scene IV

Summary: Malcolm and old Siward have come to the Birnam Wood with the English army under their command. The Scottish nobles, Menteith, Caithness, Angus, Lenox have already joined

Malcolm. Malcolm asks every soldier to cut down a branch and carry it before him. In this way, they will be able to conceal the exact size of their army and mislead enemy's spies about them. Old Siward says that the time has come for the battle which will decide who will rule over Scotland.

Critical Analysis: In this scene, we come to know the important fact that the English army commanded by Malcolm and Old Siward is advancing towards the fort of Dunsinane. Every soldier has screened himself behind the branch of a tree.

3.6.5 Act V, Scene V

Summary: At the castle of Dunsinane, Macbeth is ready to face the advancing English army. Macbeth is quite confident. Just then a sound of weeping is heard from inside. Seyton goes to find out the reason for weeping. In soliloquy, Macbeth says that he has experienced the utmost in horrors. He has got so used to murderous thought that nothing grim and terrible can shake him now. There was a time even on hearing a shriek in the night, his senses would have turned cold and his hair would have stood on ends, as if it were alive. Now nothing can startle him because he is thoroughly habituated to scenes of horror.

Seyton returns with the news that Lady Macbeth is dead. Macbeth shows little emotion on hearing this news. He says that she should have died a little later. He comments on the futility of human existence. He says that life is just a passing illusion. He also explains futility of life by saying that life is a tale told by an idiot full of sound and fury signifying nothing.

A messenger arrives who was keeping a watch on the hill, and reports that Birnam Wood is seen to move towards Dunsinane. Macbeth cannot believe that such a thing can happen. Yet it seems to him that the messenger is telling the truth. He begins to doubt the predictions made by the witches. He is also hopeful that the report given by the messenger may prove false.

Critical Analysis: In this scene, we observe that Macbeth has become hardened to scenes of horror. Macbeth receives the news of the death of his wife without any feeling. This shows that the wide distance has separated both of them. There was a time when these two were closely attached to each other. Macbeth whom we meet in this scene is completely different from the Macbeth whom we met in first two Acts. He gives the speech about the futility of human life. The messenger gives report to him that Birnam Wood is moving towards Dunsinane. Actually, it is the English soldiers who carry branches of trees in front of them while moving towards Dunsinane.

3.6.6 Act V, Scene VI

Summary: Malcolm and old Siward command the English army. They have also got support from many nobles with their soldiers. They are ready for the battle. Malcolm gives order to his soldiers to throw away the branches of the trees that were hiding them from view and reveal actual strength. He then asks old Siward to lead the first division, while he himself assisted by Macduff will do the rest. Old Siward gets ready with a feeling of confidence to fight against Macbeth.

Critical Analysis: This scene informs the audience the arrival of the forces of Malcolm near Dunsinane castle. Malcolm announces that old Siward will lead the first battle. Macduff and Malcolm will complete the encounter. This shows the idea of propriety and orderliness in Malcolm's army. Macbeth's army is devoid of discipline and devotion.

3.6.7 Act V, Scene VII

Summary: Macbeth is ready for the battle. However, he recognizes the difficult situation into which he has been forced by the enemy. He compares his condition to a bear tied to a stake. He cannot run away. He has to face the enemy. However, he feels confident because there is nobody who is not born of a woman. Young Siward appears and challenges Macbeth to fight. They fight and young Siward is killed by Macbeth.

Macduff has vowed revenge against Macbeth. He is looking for Macbeth. Macduff says that he will fight against Macbeth. He is determined to kill him. In the meantime, the castle of Dunsinane has been surrendered without any resistance. Scottish Thanes fight in support of Malcolm.

Critical Analysis: Macbeth imagines that his condition is like a baited bear. He feels that his condition has become like a captured animal, which is furious yet cannot move. He says,

"They have tied me to a stake. I cannot fly." Macbeth killed the young Siward. Macduff arrives before Macbeth. He is determined to take revenge of the massacre of his family. Old Siward yet does not know the heroic self-sacrifice of his son.

3.6.8 Act V, Scene VIII

Summary: Macbeth knows that the situation is desperate. However, he would not commit suicide, because it would be a foolish action. Macduff appears and challenges Macbeth to a fight. Macbeth however tells him that he has avoided fighting against Macduff. Because already Macbeth has a deep sense of guilt, as he ordered the murder of Macduff's family. He would not like to worsen the sense of guilt by killing Macduff. But Macduff is resolved to fight against Macbeth. Macbeth has no alternative. Macbeth now tells Macduff that his life is protected by a charm, and one born of a woman cannot kill him. Macduff replies that Macbeth should not put trust in charm in that case. Macduff reveals that he was removed from his mother's womb prematurely by means of a surgical operation, and that he is not therefore born of a woman in the normal sense. On hearing this, Macbeth curses the witches. The witches had ill-advised him by telling the prophecy with double sense. Macbeth says that there is no point in fighting against Macduff.

Macduff expresses the desire to spare Macbeth's life and to take him as a prisoner. He will afterwards exhibit him as a rare monster. But Macbeth would not like to suffer the degradation of being taken a prisoner. He puts up a fight. Macbeth is killed in this battle. The victory of Malcolm is proclaimed.

Critical Analysis: Macbeth ponders whether suicide at this point would be his better option. Macduff gives a bold challenge to Macbeth. He calls Macbeth "Hell-Hound" which confirms the true nature of the tyrant king.

Macbeth warns Macduff that he is invulnerable. Macduff now tells to Macbeth that he entered the world by being "untimely ripped" from his mother's womb. He was not therefore in the strict sense "born" of woman.

3.6.9 Act V, Scene IX

Summary: Ross brings the sad news that young Siward has been killed in the battle. Old Siward declares that even if he had a large number of sons he could not have wished them a fairer death than the one which his only son met. Young Siward died a glorious death. He died like a great soldier. Macduff carries Macbeth's head on the point of his spear while all the nobles hail Malcolm as the new King of Scotland. Malcolm expresses his gratitude to the Scottish nobles for their support. He promotes them all to the status of Earls. He promises to reward all those who were banished from their country by the tyrant, Macbeth. He would recall friends who fled to escape the trap of the tyrant. He would punish cruel ministers of the dead murderer and his devilish queen. He thanks them all at once and each one individually and invites them all to his coronation ceremony at Scone.

Critical Analysis: In the concluding scene of the play, the evil doer Macbeth is punished. We do not feel sympathy for Macbeth now, because now he has become a brute. Yet, we admire him for the courage he displays in the last scenes. We also appreciate him for his expression of feeling of repentance that he genuinely experiences when he recalls the murder of Macduff's family. His decision to die fighting in the battle instead of saving his life by offering himself as a prisoner, also shows his bravery.

Ross gives the report of the death of young Siward on the battlefield. Old Siward reacts worthy of a great military commander. He says that his son died a glorious death on the battlefield, fighting against the tyrant, Macbeth. It is pathetic scene.

Macbeth describes the witches as juggling fiends. He now realizes that they spoke in an ambiguous manner. They used deceptive language to mislead him.

Malcolm's victory symbolizes the re-emergence and re-assertion of the natural order of things. The play ends with the defeat of the evil and the victory of the good. Thus, the play offers a moral for us. Macbeth and Lady Macbeth represent the forces of evil, which have been routed. Malcolm, Macduff, and above all, the English King Edward the Confessor, represent the forces of good who have got success.

3.7 Check your Progress

(1) What role do the witches play in bringing about the downfall of Macbeth?

(2) What is dramatic irony? Give some examples from *Macbeth*.

(3) How does Malcolm authenticate Macduff's sincerity?

(4) Comment on the value and significance of the Porter scene in *Macbeth*.

(5) Write a note on the ghost of Banquo.

3.8 Key to Check your Progress

(1) For answer see 3.2.3; 3.4.5 and 3.5.1

(2) For answer see 3.2.6

(3) For answer see 3.5.3

(4) For answer see 3.3.3

(5) For answer see 3.4.4

3.9 Summary

We have studied the plot of the play. Now it is clear that Macbeth is an ambitious person. Ambition acts as a determining passion in the play. Ambition is an unreasonable desire to enjoy honours, estates, and great places. Such is the passion which moves Macbeth and Lady Macbeth to the murder of Duncan. The play is really a study in fear. Passion has created havoc in Macbeth's life. It describes superstitious fear, melancholy fear, the fear of those who share our secrets, the fear of those who are our rivals, the fear of those whom we have harmed, all the fears that lead to murder after murder. The result of these evil deeds is in melancholy, sleeplessness, disturbing dreams, ghosts and visions, sleepwalking, and self-destruction. Fears have destroyed peace and happiness in Macbeth's life; it has made ambition fruitless and success a mockery. Macbeth follows the path of evil for fulfillment of his ambition to be the king of Scotland. Three witches and Lady Macbeth instigate him for the crime. He murders Banquo, Macduff's wife and children. The nobles revolt against him. Malcolm and Macduff with old Siward, with the help of the English army invade Scotland. They get the support of many Scottish people. Macduff kills Macbeth in battle. Malcolm becomes the new king of Scotland. He is good, gracious, cautious, and shrewd man. In this way, order is established in the state. We get a glimpse of a peaceful state ruled by a shrewd and honest king.

3.10 Glossary

- Assassination—to murder somebody especially important or famous, for money or for political reasons
- Imagination—the ability to create mental images or pictures
- Irony—the expression of one's meaning by saying the direct opposite of what one is thinking but using tone of voice to indicate one's real meaning
- Prophecy—a statement that tells what will happen in the future
- Soliloquy—speaking one's thoughts aloud, especially in a play when a character does this without another character being present on stage
- Treacherous—behaving so as to betray somebody or something; intending or intended to betray somebody
- Vantage—right moment, suitable opportunity
- Reflection—return, turning back
- Sergeant—officer in an army
- Brave—noble, worthy, excellent
- Flout—insult, abuse
- Lavish—undisciplined, impetuous, wild
- Composition—settlement, truce, coming to terms
- Witches—the women thought to have evil magic powers.

3.11 Further Reading

Brooks, Cleanth. "The Naked Babe and the Cloak of Manilness." *The Well Wrought Urn: Studies in the Structure of Poetry*. 1947. San Diego: Harcourt, 1974, 22-49.

Knight, L.C. "How Many Children had Lady Macbeth? An Essay in the Theory and Practice of Shakespeare Criticism." *Explorations*. New York University Press, 1964, 15-54.

3.12 Recommended Reading

Faulkner, William. *Deconstructing "Macbeth": The Hyperontological View*. Toronto: Associate Press, 1990.

Paul, Henry N. *The Royal Play of Macbeth: When, Why, and How it was Written by Shakespeare*. New York: Macmillan, 1950.

Shakespeare, William. *Macbeth*. New Delhi: Oxford University Press, 2016.

——. *Macbeth*. ed. Clark Sandra; Mason Pamela. *The Arden Shakespeare: Macbeth*. London: 2015.

Shelley, David. *Today's Shakespeare: Macbeth*. New York: Monarch Press, 1990.

4

Characterization

4.0 Objectives

After studying this unit, you will be able:

- to understand each character in the play
- to learn the various kinds of relationships and character groupings
- to know the significant traits of the various characters and what roles they are playing in the play
- to study the technical aspects like symbolism, imagery, etc.

4.1 Introduction

In this unit, we are going to study the characters in the play. We study their behaviour in the play. We also study various traits of the characters.

4.2 Major Characters

4.2.1 Macbeth

(a) **A Complex Character:** With the exception of Hamlet, Macbeth has been considered as the most complex character Shakespeare ever portrayed. He is described as a complex character because his motives cannot be analysed and labelled. He has courage. Because of the ambition of becoming King of Scotland, he assassinated King Duncan. He becomes the king. He feels himself insecure in the position. He kills many people whom he considers the opponents and obstacles for his position. He becomes a seasoned conspirator. He does possess some better elements in his character. Sensibility and imagination are the better elements in his personality. We feel pity for Macbeth because he has elements of greatness within him; later evil dominates and conquers all that is good in him.

(b) **Ambition and Pride:** Ambition seems to have been a dominating feeling in Macbeth. Therefore, Macbeth has generally been considered a tragedy of ambition. It is a tragedy of ambition to a considerable extent. Ambition acts as a determining passion in this play. The witches have predicted monarchy for him. He has secretly been cherishing the desire for monarchy. The evil in him is symbolized by ambition. The destruction of Macbeth corresponds to the fall of Satan. Ambition was Satan's sin also. According to Lily B. Campbell, a critic, this play is a study in fear. The passion of ambition moves Macbeth and Lady Macbeth to assassinate King Duncan. Ambition is also the main reason for their downfall.

(c) **Weakness of Will:** Macbeth is certainly a great military general. He is a devoted subject to King Duncan. He deserves gratitude and praise of the king. The witches exercise influence upon him. The witches cannot exercise their power of influence upon those people who have a strong will power. A person of strong will power does not allow oneself to be seduced by evil. Lady Macbeth also exercises her influence upon him. The witches and Lady Macbeth are the agents of the evil. Macbeth surrenders himself to their influence because his will power is weak.

Macbeth has been a man of strong imagination. And a man of strong imagination cannot be completely bad. Before murdering Duncan, he saw a phantom dagger. It is an indication that the crime of murder will have horrible consequences. He also tells to Lady Macbeth that they will not proceed further in that business.

(d) **Evil Thought and It's Suppression:** When we first meet Macbeth, we already know him to be a military general of extraordinary power. He has put down a rebellion. He defeated the foreign invaders. The information given by the bleeding sergeant and by Ross and Angus show the great personal bravery and heroism of Macbeth on battlefield. Thus, he is a man who inspires fear and admiration. Duncan refers to him as 'worthy cousin' and 'noble' Macbeth. The manner in which he reacts to the prophecies of the witches is a clear indication that he has secretly been cherishing an ambition to become the king. When one of the prophecies made by the witches is fulfilled, by the conferment of the title of the Thane of Cawdor upon him, Macbeth, in an aside, regards it as a happy prologue to the fulfillment of the next prophecy, namely that he will become the king. The thought of becoming king has engrossed him. In an aside, he reveals the means which have occurred to him for attaining that position. He is thinking of assassinating the present king, Duncan to achieve the fulfillment of his secret ambition which has been stimulated by the prophecies. However, Macbeth has a strong conscience. Therefore, he tries to suppress the thoughts of ambition. In another aside, he says that if he is destined to become the king, he would attain that position without doing any effort on his part. The moment, he speaks of the horrid image is the moment of the occurrence of the evil thought in his mind. The evil is suppressed.

(e) **The Thought of Assassination of Duncan Revives in Macbeth's Mind:** Duncan greets and thanks him for rendering great services to the crown. Macbeth is a man of qualities. He is the most outstanding individual at Duncan's court. He is even greater than Duncan in some respects. However, when Duncan announced nomination of Malcolm as the heir to the throne, Macbeth in an aside says that he is still ambitious to be the king. He thinks that promotion of Malcolm is the difficulty in his way of becoming the king. He thinks of the way to attain kingship. The way he thinks of is the assassination of King Duncan. In an aside, Macbeth calls upon the stars to hide their light so that his 'black' and 'deep desires' do not become visible. It is clear therefore that he has not been able to completely discard the idea of assassination which came to him previously. He has written a letter to his wife in it he has written about witches prophecy about him.

(f) **Conscience Stronger than Ambition at First:** When Macbeth comes to home, his wife too speaks to him of the assassination of Duncan as the mean to achieve monarchy, he does not approve of the suggestion. He says, "We will speak further." In one soliloquy, he says that sad consequences overtake the evil doer. He thinks that Duncan is his kinsman, his guest, and his king, whom he should defend rather than murder. Macbeth also thinks that people will feel deep sympathy when they find that such a noble and good king has been assassinated. He is now afraid of the disastrous consequences of the assassination of King Duncan. The force of conscience is active in his mind. He tells his wife: "We will proceed no further in this business."

(g) **His Wife's Instigation for Murder:** Lady Macbeth plays a decisive role. She taunts Macbeth for his lack of courage, and also for not loving her well enough to carry out a task, which he has undertaken. She speaks to him with intense feeling and in a forceful language that Macbeth is overwhelmed and agrees to complete the task. Macbeth cannot resist his wife's arguments and words. His ambition partly plays the decisive role for the crime of assassination. Lady Macbeth's influence is predominant. If Lady Macbeth had not influenced his mind and heart, he would never have committed the murder of Duncan.

(h) **Macbeth's Self-damnation:** Murder of Duncan brings Macbeth's damnation of his self. By murdering Duncan, Macbeth strangled his own conscience. He could still have returned to the path of righteousness. His ambition and the promise he had given to wife prove stronger than his conscience. When he was entering Duncan's bed-chamber in order to murder him, his conscience opposed him by showing him an imaginary dagger His conscience does not stop him from accomplishing the task.

(i) **His Conscience after the Murder of Duncan:** Macbeth commits the murder of Duncan. But his conscience does not die. When he is coming back from the chamber after committing the murder, two people are praying, he cannot say the word 'Amen.' A voice asks him to sleep no more because he has already murdered sleep. These are the indications that he feels a keen sense of guilt after committing the horrible deed. He cannot go back to Duncan's bed chamber to put the dagger in guards' hands and smear them with Duncan's blood.

(j) **The Murder of Banquo and a Deep Sense of Guilt:** Macbeth has now taken the road to self-damnation. He is now unable to stop himself from the path of crime. He thinks that Banquo poses danger to his position, he also thinks of the witches' prophecy that Banquo's descendents will be kings. He hatches a conspiracy to kill Banquo and his son, Fleance. He thinks that he feels insecure in presence of Banquo. He orders the murderers to murder Banquo and his son Fleance. Banquo is killed, and Fleance manages to escape. This crime causes him great distress and misery. At the time of the state banquet, he sees a hallucination that Banquo is sitting in his chair, looking at him in an accusing manner. Macbeth' troubled conscience makes him see the hallucination of Banquo's ghost as previously he had seen the visionary dagger moving towards Duncan's chamber. Macbeth is at this time completely frightened by the sight of Banquo's ghost.

(k) **Moves further on the Path of Wickedness:** Macbeth sees the ghost of Banquo at the time of the banquet. It is the indication that his conscience is still working. But now he has gone beyond any moral or spiritual recovery. He tells to his wife about his apprehensions about Macduff. The very next day, he goes to the Weird Sisters to know about his future. At the time of discussion with his wife, he tells her that now he is a novice in crime but soon he will become hardened. He also feels that it is now too late for him to leave path of evil because he has already gone too far on the path of evil. There is no possibility of return to good path for him.

(l) **Away from any Chance of Moral Revival:** Macbeth consciously goes to the witches for discussion. Still, his conscience tells him to leave path of evil. But he does not give any attention to it. He has already gone beyond any possibility of moral or spiritual healing. He has gone to the witches; it shows that he is doomed. He has put complete trust in their promises and assurances. The witches advise him to beware of Macduff. After coming back from meeting the witches, he orders the ruffians to seize the castle of Macduff, and kill his wife and children. He has now become a ruthless and unscrupulous tyrant. After this Macbeth's moral fall is swift and sure. He now becomes a most despotic and tyrannical king. Now people of Scotland witness a reign of terror. He has lost his sensibility. Even the news of his wife's death leaves him unmoved. He also realizes the futility of his life. He compares his life to the yellow leaf in autumn. He only thinks of his personal safety. He feels confident because he believes in the witches' prophecy that anyone who is born of a woman will not do any harm to him. Soon he gets the report that the Birnam Wood is moving towards Dunsinane. Soon he comes to know that the witches had used deceptive language to mislead him. Finally, Macduff kills him in the battle. Macduff was not born of a woman in the normal sense. He was taken out of his mother's womb prematurely by caesarian operation.

Macbeth differs from other Shakespearean heroes like Othello, Hamlet, and King Lear. We admire other heroes till the end. This is not true of Macbeth. Their essential nobility does not suffer any deteriorating at any stage. We feel sympathy for Macbeth, but we do not admire him because of his criminal deeds. Macbeth is a hero who afterwards becomes a villain. In the battle, he is killed by Macduff. We feel that poetic justice has been done. We also feel pity for him, because he had so many good qualities in him, but he brought his own downfall by following the path of evil. Had he remained on the path of virtue, he would have remained an admiring and tremendously successful person in the important position. Macbeth murders King Duncan, and becomes the king. His crime does not stop here. To secure his position of power, he murders Banquo, then Macduff's wife and children. If he had obeyed his imagination, he would have been safe.

In Act V, Scene V, Macbeth refers to a time which shows Macbeth's native disposition. Macbeth says that there was a time he would have felt chilled, on hearing a shriek at night. Now he has become habituated with the deeds of horror. He knows the essential wickedness of the deed. This conscience holds him back. The man, who has slaughtered the enemy soldiers, would hardly be frightened by blood or consequences. He thinks of Duncan as his guest, kinsman, and king. Therefore, he considers that his duty is to protect the king. Even when he has been hardened and coarsened by crime, he cannot repress the imagination in him.

4.2.2 Lady Macbeth

(a) **Similarity in Passion:** Macbeth and Lady Macbeth are two terrible figures in the play, *Macbeth*. These two characters inspire feeling of awe. Both of them are influenced by the passion of ambition. Both of them are high, commanding, and proud. They are selfish. They do not think beyond their aim of power and position. The difference between the two is that she is not deterred by scruples, as she is more impulsive. Her husband is more thoughtful and imaginative. Lady Macbeth has been compared as another Witch, more diabolical. She possesses the gracious human form, with irresistible valour to tongue. Lady Macbeth instigates her husband to the act of murder. She gets an ascendency over him because of his weakness of will. Had he possessed strong will power, perhaps he would have resisted her instigation. His weakness of will is temperamental.

(b) **Lady Macbeth's Influence on her Husband:** We first meet Lady Macbeth when she is reading a letter sent by her husband about his meeting with the witches and their prophecy about his future. Lady Macbeth has already been harbouring the ambition that her husband should be the king. She thinks that the way for him to get the throne is to kill the present king. She thinks that her husband is too kind to do the evil deed of murder. She plays a determining role in the course of events in the play.

(c) **A Woman of Compact Resolution:** When Lady Macbeth completes reading of a letter sent by her husband, a messenger arrives and informs her that King Duncan is arriving at her castle that very night to stay as a guest. She removes his doubts regarding the act of murder. She instigates him with the word, 'Coward' which no soldier will tolerate. It is her plan to put the blame on the guards who stand outside the bed chamber of Duncan. She does not lose her self-control after the murder of Duncan, and also in the banquet scene.

(d) **Partly Lacks Pity and Humanity:** Lady Macbeth is dreadful and inhuman. She does not feel any sense of pity while thinking of the conspiracy of assassinating King Duncan. Partly she possesses the pity. She tells that if Duncan did not resemble her father as he slept, she would have herself committed the murder. She does not recognize the value for the lives of the guards, the blame of murder was put upon them. Macbeth knew that they would plead their innocence, therefore, Macbeth killed them. She does not care for the condemnation or hatred of the world. She walks in the sleep, and while walking she talks about the murder of Duncan, Banquo, and Macduff's family, it shows her guilty conscience. Had she been thoroughly inhuman, she would not have suffered from somnambulism.

(e) **Her Essential Feminine Nature:** Lady Macbeth has been ambitious, and she instigates her husband for crime of murder. She reproaches him for his lack of courage, challenges his love. She takes the initiative. Then he becomes ready to accomplish the task. She is the impulsive woman. She says:

> The raven himself is hoarse
> That croaks the fatal entrance of Duncan
> Under my battlements. Come, you spirits
> That tends on mortal thoughts, unsex me here,
> And fill me, from the crown to the toe, top-full
> Of direst cruelty! make thick my blood,
> Stop up the access and passage to remorse
> That no compunctious visitings of nature
> Shake my fell purpose, nor keep peace between
> The effect and it! Come to my woman's breasts,
> And take my milk for gall, you murdering ministers,
> Wherever in your sightless substances
> You wait on nature's mischief!

She prays to the powers of evil that she may be unsexed. This has been temporary. The woman in her asserts in course of time. She says that if Duncan had not resembled her father in his sleep, she would have killed him herself.

(f) **Her Love for her Husband:** Lady Macbeth is not a depraved woman. It is her love for her husband which leads her to the path of crime. She knows her husband well. She knows that he is ambitious, but he lacks the will and the wickedness to realize his ambition. She takes the initiative in the task, so that her husband's ambition may be fulfilled. He appeals the evil spirits to unsex her to make her cruel to accomplish the task. She overstrains herself, for the sake of her husband. The result is a total breakdown. However cruel she becomes, she cannot renounce her womanly nature. After the first crime, she keeps herself apart from her husband. She suffers in loneliness. Lady

Macbeth is not a bad woman. She sacrificed herself for the sake of her husband.

(g) **Her Resourcefulness:** Lady Macbeth is a resourceful woman, compared to her husband. She hatches the conspiracy for the murder of Duncan. She helps Macbeth to carry out the conspiracy. After committing the murder, Macbeth loses control over himself. He is tormented by imaginative terrors. She comes to help him in this critical time. After murdering Duncan, Macbeth had brought the dagger with him. Macbeth shudders to go back to the chamber to put back the daggers. Lady Macbeth goes to the bed-chamber to put the daggers there. After the incident, Macbeth loses control over himself. At this critical moment Lady Macbeth comes to his help. Otherwise Macbeth might have betrayed himself, when he meets Banquo and Lennox in the morning. At the State Banquet scene Macbeth saw the ghost of Banquo, sitting in his chair, no other person saw the ghost, Lady Macbeth saves the situation by telling that this type of behaviour is usual with him from the very youth. She saves him from self-betrayal.

(h) **Her Nervous Breakdown:** After accomplishing the task, she remains a firm and determined woman for a time being. Her expectations are not realized after completion of the task. She expected success, glory greatness in her life. Instead of that the ruin of the land and husband takes place. Her spirit sinks. She resists the suffering in a heroic manner. She suffers from somnambulism. While walking in the sleep, she is reminded of the scenes of murder of Duncan, Banquo, Macduff's wife and children. Her guilty conscience rebukes her. Earlier she thought a little water will clear them of the deed, now she thinks that smell and stain of blood will never wash away.

(i) **Discussion about the Witches:** In the banquet scene, when the guests have gone, Macbeth expresses his apprehensions about Macduff. Lady Macbeth asks him whether he had sent for that man. He replies that he will do so soon. He then informs her about his plan to go the witches to meet and find out something more about his future. He also tells her that he has gone too far on the path of crime that he cannot return. Lady Macbeth tells him that he needs sleep, nature's medicine for all ills. He says that soon he will become a hardened person in shedding the blood, though now he is a novice.

(j) **Her Death a Little Concern to him:** Macbeth has become so hardened that he does not move by the news of his wife's death. When report is given to him about her death, he replies that she should have died later. There would have been a better time to receive such news. Then he comments on the futility of human life. He says that life is an illusion, a person a wretched actor, life is a tale told by an idiot, full of idle pain and rage, and little meaning in it. He is fed up with life, so his wife's death does not move him.

Lady Macbeth is a woman of strong will power and determination. In the early part of the play her role is evil. She instigates her husband for the crime. But ultimately she suffers from the sense of guilt. She is an exceptional woman. She sacrifices her life for the sake of her husband.

4.2.3 Banquo

Banquo is a foil to Macbeth. King Duncan praises both of them for their valour in battle. But it is clear that the king honours Macbeth above Banquo. Certainly, Macbeth appears to be the more dominating person. Banquo must have served to increase Macbeth's renown by being placed beside him.

Macbeth is greeted by the witches on the wild heath, and they promise him monarchy in future. Then Banquo gets interested and asks the witches whether they have anything to tell about his future. Banquo addresses the witches in a lighthearted manner, and not seriously as Macbeth does. Banquo cautions Macbeth that the witches may not be believed, because they tell truth about trifles, and tempt to do the crime which may lead to damnation. Banquo is loyal to the king. He keeps his innocence and virtue untainted.

Macbeth secures the throne of Scotland. Banquo seems to know by which way he might have secured the throne. He thinks of the prophecy:

> Thou hast it now: king, Cawdor, Glamis, all,
> As the weird women promised, and I fear
> Thou play'dst most foully for't; yet it was said

It should not stand in thy posterity,
But that myself should be the root and father
Of many kings. If there come truth from them–
As upon thee, Macbeth, their speeches shine–
Why, by the verities on thee made good,
May they not be my oracles as well,
And set me up in hope? But, hush; no more.

(a) **A Honest Person:** The witches greet him as the founder of a dynasty. He has not taken their prophecy seriously. He has no inclination towards crime, therefore he does not think of witches so often like Macbeth. He neither begs favour from them, nor is he afraid of them. He tells to Macbeth frankly the consequences of trusting them. He does allow the witches to contaminate his mind or soul. But after all, Banquo is also a human being. He confesses that cursed thoughts come to his mind in sleep. He is honest and faithful; therefore, he controls those thoughts.

(b) **His Cautious Nature:** Banquo is brave by nature, and soldier by profession. He is also a shrewd man of the world. He knows by what ways Macbeth has secured the throne. But he keeps Macbeth in good humour. Yet, he does not do anything against his own conscience. He does his best to avert suspicion. He expresses his loyalty to the king. Banquo's caution creates awe and admiration.

(c) **His Modest Nature:** Modesty is the important characteristic of Banquo's nature. He has an equal share in winning the battle of Fife. King showered praise and extravagant title upon Macbeth. Banquo is contented with the embrace from the king. King praises him that he has shown equal fortitude on battlefield. He gives a modest reply to the king: "There if I grow, the harvest is your own."

(d) **His Integrity:** Banquo tells to Macbeth that last night he dreamt three Weird Sisters. Their prophecy about Macbeth proves partly true. Macbeth asks him whether Banquo will support him when the time comes. He gives the answer that he will support Macbeth in any honourable course of action. This shows Banquo's integrity and loyalty to the king.

(e) **Macbeth's View of Banquo:** Macbeth knows well that Banquo is a person of modest and royal nature. He also knows that Banquo is a wise person whose valour is guided by his wisdom. In the presence of Banquo, Macbeth feels uneasy, because his conscience is rebuked, just as Mark Antony's was rebuked in Caesar's presence. Macbeth also knows that it was Banquo who first spoke to the witches. The witches had told the prophecy that Banquo' descendents will be the kings. Macbeth thinks that he has committed the bloody deed for the benefit of Banquo's children.

(f) **Contrast to Macbeth:** Banquo contrasts to Macbeth in many respects. Banquo is loyal to the king, whereas Macbeth behaved most treacherously with the king. Banquo is a person with great integrity. Macbeth becomes depraved and degraded under the influence of his ambition. Macbeth is jealous of Banquo's moral superiority. When he comes to know that with the case of Macbeth, the witches' prophecy proved true, he thinks that with regard to him also prophecy may come true. When Banquo and Macbeth meet the three witches, he points out the evil nature of the witches.

Banquo is a brave, shrewd, practical and self-controlled man. He does not lack worldly ambition; he merely disdains the evil methods to achieve it. He is a loyal subject and a brave general who follows the path of integrity.

4.2.4 Macduff

Macduff is a nobleman of Scotland. He is an outspoken soldier, and a patriot. He is noble, wise and clear sighted person. He is the victorious opponent of Macbeth. When he fled to England, his family was massacred by Macbeth. Out of patriotic zeal, and with the motive of personal revenge, he killed Macbeth in the battle.

(a) **His Patriotism:** Macduff suspects Macbeth from the very beginning. When Macbeth confesses that he killed the two chamberlains, he challenges him: "Wherefore did you so?" It shows that he is a very spirited person. When Banquo expresses the determination to discover and fight the traitors, it is Macduff who seconds it.

He refuses to attend Macbeth's coronation ceremony. His loyalty to Duncan prevents him from expressing his allegiance to the usurper. His patriotism warns him that he should not be committed to a tyrant. He openly defies and protests Macbeth. He flatly refuses to attend the state banquet to which Macbeth invites him. When Banquo is murdered, he resolves to free the country from the clutches of Macbeth's tyranny. Macbeth's reign has become a reign of terror and fear. People felt insecure. He goes to England and meets Malcolm there. He describes the condition of terror and horror in Scotland in a graphic manner to Malcolm. He urges Malcolm to take arms against Macbeth. While going to England, he leaves his wife and children at the mercy of the tyrant. Tyrant mercilessly kills them. Ross informs him that his family was killed. In the battle, he fights with the only one aim that is to kill Macbeth. He accomplishes his task.

(b) **His Uncommunicativeness:** Macduff is a man of action, not a man of words. This explains why he had left his family without giving them any explanation. In conversation with Malcolm, he describes in the graphic manner the horrible condition in Scotland. While in England he learns that his family had been killed. A personal motive is added to his patriotic motive. He recognizes now that he has been very negligent to the security and welfare of his family. He is filled with self-reproach.

(c) **An Agent of Retribution:** It is Macduff who slays Macbeth in the battlefield. Macduff reveals to Macbeth that he is not the person born of a woman in the normal sense of the term. He proves to be an agent of retribution against Macbeth. Thus, Macduff belongs to the group of characters who represent goodness in the play. Macbeth and Lady Macbeth represent evil in the play. Because of political situation in the country, and for the purpose of secrecy he could not inform his family about his visit to England. He loves his family well. In the time of crisis, he proved negligent regarding family responsibility.

(d) **Lady Macduff's Reaction:** Lady Macduff is a noble minded woman. She does not understand the motive of her husband in fleeing the country. She does not hesitate to call him a traitor to his family. She describes her son to Ross: "Fathered he is, and yet he's fatherless." Her conversation with her son reflects the pathetic condition of the family in absence of Macduff. Thus, pathos reaches its climax when ruffians kill her son; they chase her and kill her. Her speech, just before murderers burst upon her and her son, reflects the truth:

But I remember now
I am in this earthly world; where to do harm
Is often laudable; to do good sometime
Accounted dangerous folly

(e) **His Affection for Family:** Lady Macduff has questioned her husband's affection and the strength of his family attachment. But Ross brings him the news of the slaughter of his wife and children, in his castle, when he was not there to protect them, his grief first tongue-tied. He considered himself failed to protect his family in his absence. He is determined to take revenge upon the murderer. His broken sentences, his repetition of the questions already answered show a veteran soldier full of affection for the children and wife. He resolves to avenge their death with his own hands.

4.2.5 King Duncan

King Duncan is a noble, gracious king of Scotland. He is an honourable and virtuous leader. The historical Duncan was weak and incompetent ruler. Shakespeare depicts him worthy of the all veneration and loyalty of his subjects. He is of a kind temperament. Macbeth is aware of Duncan's virtues and sees the enormity of his proposed murder of Duncan:

This Duncan
Hath born his faculties so meek, hath been
So clear in his great office, that his virtues
Will plead like angels, trumpet-tongued, against
The deep damnation of his taking off.

He is quick to punish those who have done treason. He is quick to reward those who have shown great courage and heroism in defeating the traitors. He punished treacherous Macdonwald. Duncan praises Macbeth for his bravery and calls him a 'noble kinsman.' He also rewards him and bestows upon him the title of Thane of Cawdor. To appreciate his services, he honours him by becoming his guest for the night.

Malcolm describes him, "as a most sainted king." He has all the essential qualities of a king. He is holy, generous, just, and quick both in punishing and rewarding. He quickly orders the execution of the Thane of Cawdor for his treachery, and he is quick to reward Macbeth by declaring him as the new Thane of Cawdor.

He is trustful. He has been betrayed by one in whom he had kept absolute trust. Yet, he does not hesitate to place his life in the hands of another favourite. He is a man of refined nature. He does not use strict measures to keep check over his ambitious nobles. He declares nomination of Macbeth as the heir to the throne. He cannot guess that there are other aspirants to the throne. He fails to penetrate the mask of Lady Macbeth's treachery. He thinks nothing wrong in Macbeth's absence from the supper table. He even enjoys himself heartily and distributes presents all around. It is this failure to understand the world, this hermit-like saintliness of him which cost him his life.

4.2.6 Malcolm

Malcolm is a cool, wise, visionary man. He is richly endowed with all the qualities that are essential for a leader. He seems to be a contrast to his father, Duncan. He is on his guard and cautious. Duncan is unsuspecting and trustful. He has learnt the lesson of cautiousness through experience. He runs away and seeks shelter in England immediately after the assassination of his father. He has to resist the seductions of Macbeth. He has to keep himself out of the trap Macbeth lays for him. He rightly says that "modest wisdom plucks me from over credulous haste." The wicked Macbeth has often tried to entrap him by sending messengers with false declarations of love and friendship. He has to be a little cautious in his own interest. His experience has taught him to first validate a person's loyalty and then believe in a person. Constant alertness is his leading attribute. He describes himself in dark colours in order to test Macduff's loyalty. When he is convinced of Macduff's sincerity, he retracts his self-accusation. He is truthful, honest and sincere. He is a slave of neither lust nor avarice. He is deeply grateful to the English King, Edward, the Confessor.

Malcolm does not seem to be gifted with the finer sensibilities. He can hardly express concern over Macbeth's grief. He does not seem to have enough gracefulness to respect this grief. He talks of great revenge at that time, which is ill-suited. He is not free from rash optimism.

When marching to Dunsinane, he looks forward to triumph and rejoicing, for this he is promptly, though gently rebuked by the veteran warriors, Siward and Macduff. After the battle, nobles acclaim him as the King of Scotland. He seems to be in immoderate hurry to make himself even with his supporters. He perhaps has not been able to know that they fought for other motives than just the rewards.

Malcolm is a promising and hopeful king. It is he who orders his soldiers to conceal themselves with the boughs from the Birnam Wood. Macbeth's confidence is shaken, when he gets the messenger reports him that Birnam Wood is moving to Dunsinane. Malcolm has got victory over Macbeth in the battle. His speech at the end of the play shows him to be young, efficient, and good. His coronation restores peace, truth and legitimate kingship to Scotland. He has destroyed evil and disorder in Scotland. He has restored order, peace, and harmony in the country. We get the indication that he proves to be a competent, honest, and shrewd king.

4.3 Minor Characters

4.3.1 Ross

Ross does not take prominent part in the action of the drama. But he is present at every important scene. He is not a strong personality that might influence the behaviour of others. Yet, he is a necessary link in the sequence of events that compose the play. He does not possess the initiative or strength of character. He also does not have any selfish motive or vices. He enjoys the confidence of three kings, Duncan, Macbeth, and Malcolm.

Ross is the man who brings to Lady Macduff the news that her husband has fled from Scotland. When Lady Macduff accuses her husband for acting in an irresponsible manner, and having no love for them, Ross defends him, describes him as 'noble, wise, judicious.' Seeing Lady Macduff's distress, Ross is moved to deep sympathy, and is almost in tears. It is Ross who informs Malcolm and Macduff, who are at this time in Scotland, of the distressing conditions that prevail in Scotland under Macbeth's rule.

In the course of the description of the misery of Scotland, he says that it cannot be called our mother but our grave. He is the person who reveals to Macduff the painful news of the slaughter of his family by the Macbeth. This news whets Macduff's anger against Macbeth, and he resolves to avenge upon the dictator. It is Ross who tells old Siward the tragic news of the death of his young son on the battlefield.

Ross, Angus, and Lenox fill the gap in the dialogue. They keep us informed about the general perception of the people about Macbeth's sovereignty in Scotland. Ross gives news of the victory at Fife to Duncan. He gives news to Malcolm that Scotland is ready for revolution.

4.3.2 Lady Macduff

Lady Macduff is a typical domestic woman. She is little concerned with the issues of state. Her thoughts range within the narrow circle—her husband, children, and the family property. Her husband has told nothing about the troubles of the state, or about Macbeth's tyranny and oppression.

Her rational mind tells her that when life and property is not safe in Scotland, the decision of her husband to go to England is a foolish act. She does not understand that if her husband is not a traitor, why he should run away from that country, and risk being considered a traitor.

When she learns of her husband's flight, she has felt the perception of danger. She is a sensible woman who talks to her child in a playful manner but she masks her forebodings. A messenger comes and warns Lady Macduff of immediate danger. She has little experience of the world; therefore in the situation of immediate peril, she does not know what to do. The ruffians arrive, they first kill her child and later they pursue her and kill her. Both mother and son fall victims to Macbeth's willful cruelty.

4.3.3 Three Witches

The three witches play the role of evil agents in the drama. They are described as the 'Weird Sisters' by various characters in the play. They lure Macbeth to perform the evil actions. The witches' beards, strange potions, and rhymed speech make them seem slightly ridiculous. They are clearly the most dangerous characters in the play. They are immensely powerful and completely wicked. Shakespeare keeps the witches outside the limits of human comprehension. They embody an unreasoning, instinctive evil. All their prophecies do not come true. The witches bear a cord resemblance to fate.

We meet the witches in the very beginning of the play, *Macbeth*. They exert a profound influence over events in the play. They introduce the play. It is a dark and dangerous play. The play deals with the theme of evil predominantly. The witches say, "Fair is foul and foul is fair." These words appear to contradict each other. Everything is not what it seems to be. These words introduce the idea of illusion and reality. The witches are deceptive, manipulating, and equivocating. Macbeth does not recognize this aspect in the early part of the play. The witches betray Macbeth. Relationships are important and they affect the lives of the people. The predestined relationship between Macbeth and three witches make it a tragedy. The relationship seems to be solid in the beginning, but later it becomes clear that it is futile from the very beginning. The witches arrange a show of apparitions for Macbeth. It is the evil scheme devised by the witches to lure Macbeth further to the path of evil. The apparitions create in Macbeth a sense of security which proves dangerous for Macbeth. It proves true in one sense that security is the mortal's chiefest enemy. He believes in the prophecy of the witches that no one will defeat him till the Birnam Wood moves to Dunsinane. He also feels secure because of the prophecy that anyone born of woman will not be able to kill him. Macduff is the person who is born through caesarian. In the normal sense, he is not born of a woman. The British army under the leadership of Malcolm, Old Siward and Macduff approaches near Dunsinane to defeat Macbeth. Malcolm orders every soldier to cut the branch of a tree and keep before oneself so that the enemy spies will not know the exact number of their soldiers. The scene of British army appears as if Birnam Wood is moving to Dunsinane. Macduff kills Macbeth in the civil war. Macbeth is doomed because of his overambitious nature and also because of his fatal association with the agents of evil. The three witches exert a considerable influence over the actions described in the play.

4.4 Check your Progress

(1) Sketch the character of Macbeth. What are his distinctive characteristics?

(2) "Lady Macbeth is not ambitious for herself, but for her husband." Justify.

(3) "Banquo is a foil to Macbeth." Substantiate.

(4) Sketch the character of Macduff. What role does he perform in the play, *Macbeth*?

(5) Write a note on the character of King Duncan.

(6) Sketch the character of Malcolm. What are the features of his character which strike you most?

(7) What role does Ross perform in the play, *Macbeth*?

(8) Sketch the character of Lady Macduff?

(9) What role do three witches play in *Macbeth*?

4.5 Key to Check your Progress

(1) For answer see 4.2.1

(2) For answer see 4.2.2

(3) For answer see 4.2.3

(4) For answer see 4.2.4

(5) For answer see 4.2.5

(6) For answer see 4.2.6

(7) For answer see 4.3.1

(8) For answer see 4.3.2

(9) For answer see 4.3.3

4.6 Summary

We have studied the major and minor character in the play. We also tried to understand the passion of ambition which leads Macbeth to the path of damnation and downfall. The passion of ambition moves Macbeth and Lady Macbeth to the assassination of King Duncan. We also have studied the impact of fear on Macbeth and Lady Macbeth. A group of characters represent goodness; another group of characters represent evil, in the world. The good wins over the evil in the concluding part of the play. Lady Macduff and her son are innocent; they suffer even if they do not harm to anyone. Banquo is honest, loyal but he is murdered because Macbeth feels insecure in his presence, he also thinks that throne should not pass to Banquo's decedents. Ross informs the important characters about the events and happenings in the state. Had Macbeth not been influenced by the three witches, he would not have become a criminal protagonist.

4.7 Glossary

- Conspire—to make secret plan with others to do something illegal or harmful
- Nomination—to propose formally that somebody should be chosen for a position
- Conscience—a person's awareness of right and wrong with regard to her or his own thought and actions
- Hallucination—the belief that one is seeing or hearing somebody or something when no such person or thing is actually present
- Apprehension—anxiety about something in the future; fear that something will be unpleasant or something unpleasant will happen
- Diabolical—very bad or annoying
- Torment—severe physical or mental suffering
- Somnambulism—the activity or habit of walking around while one I asleep
- Massacre—the killing of a large number of people.

4.8 Further Reading

Knight, Wilson. *The Imperial Theme: Further Interpretations of Shakespeare's Tragedies including the Roman Plays.* Abingdon: Routledge, 2011.

Rogers, Pat. *The Oxford Illustrated History of English Literature.* Oxford: Oxford University Press, 2013.

4.9 Recommended Reading

Dobson, Michael and Wells, Stanley (Eds.). Sharpe, Will. Sullivan, Erin. Rev. *The Oxford Companion to Shakespeare.* Oxford: Oxford University Press, 2015.

Dutton, Richard. *William Shakespeare: A Literary Life.* Basingstoke: Palgrave Macmillan, 1996.

Holbrook, Peter and Edmondson, Paul. *Shakespeare's Creative Legacies: Artists, Writers, Performers, Readers.* London: Bloomsbury Arden Shakespeare, 2016.

Lohse, Rebecca. *Lady Macbeth, King Duncan and the Witches: Why are the Characters of Shakespeare's Macbeth Still Discussed Today?* Munich: Grin Verlag, 2016.

Vivo, Alessandro. *William Shakespeare: An Analysis of Macbeth's Character.* Munich: Grin Verlag, 2013.

5

Themes

5.0 Objectives

After studying this unit you will be able:

- to study the major themes of the play
- to understand that a drama deals with a group of themes
- to understand human relationships in political terms
- to understand the relation between passion and action

5.1 Introduction

In this unit, we study the major themes of the play and learn how the play deals with many themes at the same time. Ambition, fear, appearance and reality, order and disorder are the prominent themes of the play.

5.2 Ambition

Ambition is the main theme of the play, *Macbeth*. When ambition is unchecked by moral constraints, the destruction is formed. Macbeth is a courageous Scottish general who is not naturally inclined to commit evil deeds. Yet, he has strong desire for power and advancement. He kills Duncan against his better judgment. Afterwards, he suffers from guilt and fear. Towards the end of the play, he descends into boastful madness.

Lady Macbeth is a woman of strong determination. She also cannot withstand the consequences of the immoral act. She is one of the most powerful female characters drawn by William Shakespeare. She instigates Macbeth to murder king Duncan. She reminds him that he had the courage to plan murder, when time and place was not suitable. If he performs the deed, she tells him that he will prove more of a man. She describes murder as a heroic action to him.

Macbeth and his wife both of them are driven by ambition to commit the horrible crime of the assassination of the king. Macbeth has used the violent mean to fulfill his ambition of getting monarchy of Scotland. The play has raised the problem that if one once decides to use violence for realization of power, it is difficult to stop. He is led to wicked thoughts by the prophecy of three witches. The witches' prophecy regarding 'he will become Thane of Cawdor' comes true. Macbeth is a brave soldier and a powerful man, but he is not virtuous. He is tempted to murder King Duncan for fulfillment of his ambition of becoming the king. After becoming the king, he continues with his path of crime. He feels his position insecure in presence of Banquo; he kills him by hired murderers. Banquo was a virtuous man. Macbeth is better suited to the battlefield. He lacks the necessary skill to rule without being a tyrant.

There are always potential threats to the throne. Macbeth considers, Banquo, Fleance, and Macduff, threat to his position of power. He gets tempted to use the way of violence. Usually, *Macbeth* has been regarded as a tragedy of ambition. Ambition does act as a determining passion in the play. The *French Academie* described Ambition is "an unreasonable desire to enjoy honour, estates, and great places." This passion of ambition moves Macbeth and Lady Macbeth to the murder of Duncan. The play deals with ambition as one of the themes.

5.3 Kingship and Natural Order

Macbeth is set in a society where honour to one's word and one's superiors is considered absolute. King is at the top of this hierarchy, he is considered God's representative on earth. Loyalty is an important characteristic of all human relationships, comradeship in warfare, and hospitality of host towards guest, loyalty between husband and wife. In the play, all this social relationship are broken or perverted. Lady Macbeth's domination over her husband, Macbeth's treacherous act of killing the king, breaking the bond with the companion, Banquo, and the family, all these incidents go against the natural order.

The medieval or renaissance world view saw a relationship between the order in microcosmic and macrocosmic world.

Microcosm reflects order on earth, macrocosm means there is order at the level of large-scale universe. Lenox and the Old man talk about the terrifying alteration in the natural order of the universe, tempests, earthquakes, and darkness at noon. These are the reflections which correspond to Macbeth's breaking of the order in his natural microcosmic world. Duncan's murder corresponds to the disorder in nature. Macbeth's tyranny represents the disorder in country. Malcolm establishes the order fighting a war against him.

5.4 Fear

Passion affects Macbeth and Lady Macbeth. Ambition moves them to rash deeds. Fear gradually dissolves in both of them. One leads to final self-destruction, the other to the final fury of self-despair.

Macbeth and Banquo meet the three witches on the wild heath. It is Banquo who challenges the witches, Macbeth echoes feebly his questions. Bold Banquo asks them questions whether they are real or fantastical. Fear appears in Macbeth as just as rash military courage appears in him on the battlefield.

Duncan bestows the title Prince of Cumberland upon young Malcolm. When Duncan nominates Malcolm as the heir to the throne, there is conflict within Macbeth between ambition and fear:

> The Prince of Cumberland! That is a step
> On which I must fall down, or else o'erleap
> For in my way it lies. Stars hide your fires;
> Let not light see my black and deep desires;
> The eye winks at the hand; yet let that be
> Which the eye fears, when it is done, to see.

The conflict of fear and ambition always characterizes Macbeth. He fears heaven's justice. He thinks that Duncan is his king, kinsman, and the guest. He knows that Duncan is a gracious and virtuous king. For the time being ambition loses the argument. Macbeth declares: We will proceed no further in this business.

We see first sign of fear in Lady Macbeth when she admits that she would herself have killed Duncan had he not resembled her father as he slept. It is an admission of weakness. Her courage is a type of false courage, achieved by drink. Her fear is more active and evident. Macbeth tells her he has committed the murder. Now he has killed sleep also. She asks him to wash his hands. She carries back the daggers to king's chambers and smears the grooms with blood. She fears that suspicion may fall upon them.

Macbeth is a study in the complementary pair of passions, of rash courage and fear. It begins with the courage that is not real courage and ends with the courage that is not real courage. It portrays in turn the military courage of Macbeth, his excited valour and excessive bravery in action, the drunken courage of Lady Macbeth, the bravery of passion, the fury of despair, and the courage of desperation. It pictures as well superstitious fear, melancholy fear, the fear of those who share our secrets, the fear of those who are our rivals, the fear of those whom we have harmed, all the fears that lead to murder after murder. The result is in melancholy, in sleeplessness, in disturbing dreams, in ghost and visions, in fits of passion, in frenzy, in sleep-walking, in self-destruction. Such fears destroy peace and happiness and honour and hope; fears that make ambition fruitless and success a mockery.

The play is also a study of man and woman. Lady Macbeth destroys womanliness in her. She becomes a courageous and determined woman. She becomes cruel. Even more than Macbeth she is determined to do evil. She dyes her will in her ambition. Her will is strong, and directed by passion and not reason. Her punishment is more terrible than that of Macbeth. She commits the horrible sin of self-destruction.

Macbeth is, however, not only a study of fear; it is a study in fear. The sounds and images in the play create the atmosphere of terror and fear. The incantation of the witches, the bell that tolls while Duncan dies, the cries of Duncan, the cries of the women as Lady Macbeth dies, the owl, the knocking at the gate, the wild horses that ate each other, the quaking of the earth—all of these are accompaniments of the fearful in literature.

5.5 Appearance and Reality

Distinction between appearance and reality is one of the important themes of the play. It is emphasized in the play that things are not what they seem to be. There is complete loss of values. The witches say: "Fair is foul and foul is fair." Macbeth, while describing the day, says that he has not seen so fair and foul a day.

We come to notice this theme when Duncan says that Thane of Cawdor appeared to be so honest and loyal, but he behaved in the treacherous manner in reality:

> There is no art
> To find the mind's construction in the face.
> He was a gentleman on whom I built
> An absolute trust–

The King Duncan does not realize that the new Thane of Cawdor is as treacherous as the preceding one.

When Duncan reaches Macbeth's castle in Inverness, he makes a wholesome praise of the atmosphere. He says that atmosphere in the castle is heavenly, soothing. It is mere appearance; in reality it is entirely different. It is not a heaven, but it is a hell. He does not realize that he will be murdered that very night in the same castle. The porter thinks that he is porter at the gate of hell. It is the incoherent talking of a drunkard. But it is true all the same. Macbeth's castle has become hell because of the couple's unrestrained desire for power and glory. They have murdered their king who was their monarch, kinsman, and a guest who was also a benefactor. In life also appearance and reality differ as they do in literary works.

5.6 Equivocation

The theme of equivocation appears in the very beginning of the play. The witches are equivocating fiends. They speak in such a manner to hide the truth and mislead the people. The statement which they make can be interpreted in more than one way.

The Weird Sisters tell Macbeth that he need not fear till Birnam Wood moves to Dunsinane, and no man born of a woman can do any harm to him. In this way, Macbeth is deceived. He gets in the trap of false security. However, when it is too late Macbeth realizes that the prophecy made by witches is deceptive. Appearances are deceptive. Birnam Wood appears to move but in reality it was the movement of the army under the leadership of Malcolm, the branches of the trees are used by the army in front of them to hide their numbers.

Ultimately, it is Macduff who kills Macbeth. Macduff is the man not born of a woman in the real sense of the term. He was taken out of his mother's womb through a caesarian operation. The words of the witches had given Macbeth a different meaning. He had considered himself invincible. But the hope was deceptive. Their words were equivocating. They deceived him by their ambiguous words.

King Duncan's greeting by Lady Macbeth is another example of equivocation. Outwardly she behaves as if she is the ideal hostess. Everything that she and her husband call theirs, she says, actually belongs to Duncan. Indeed, Lady Macbeth professes the greatest possible loyalty to Duncan. But in reality she has already resolved to murder King Duncan. Macbeth is the character equivocal in nature. He declares loyalty to Duncan and afterwards assassinates him with his own hands. He flatters Banquo and afterwards murders him by hired murderers. In the play, there appears contrast between appearance and reality. Macbeth shows himself to be a magnificent person, but in reality he is an evil doer.

5.7 Check your Progress

(1) Write a note on theme of ambition in Macbeth.

(2) "The theme of *Macbeth* is imposition of order on disorder." Elaborate.

(3) Lily Campbell says that "Macbeth is a study in fear." Substantiate.

(4) How does theme of appearance and reality mirror in *Macbeth*?

(5) How has equivocation been dealt as one of the leading themes in *Macbeth*?

5.8 Key to Check your Progress

(1) For answer see 5.2
(2) For answer see 5.3
(3) For answer see 5.4
(4) For answer see 5.5
(5) For answer see 5.6

5.9 Summary

The play *Macbeth* deals with the themes of ambition and fear. Macbeth is also a tragedy of ambition. Ambition does act as a determining passion in the play. The passion of ambition moves Macbeth and Lady Macbeth to assassinate King Duncan. But the play is a study in fear. It describes the complementary pair of passions rash courage and fear. It describes the fears that lead to murder after murders; the effects are in melancholy, sleeplessness, sleep walking, and self-destruction. Fears destroy happiness and honour. Fears have made ambition fruitless and success a mockery. Macbeth deals with the atmosphere of terror and fear. It also depicts the themes of equivocation, kingship and order, the issues which are integral part of a society.

5.10 Glossary

- Appearance—the act of becoming visible or noticeable
- Fear—to be afraid of somebody or something
- Equivocation—to talk about something in a way that is deliberately not clear in order to hide the truth or mislead people
- Hierarchy—chain of command
- Microcosm—a thing or place or community regarded as representing on a small scale something very much larger
- Macrocosm—the universe, any large complete structure containing smaller structures
- Tyranny—the unfair, severe or cruel use of power or authority.

5.11 Further Reading

Richardson, William. *Essays on Shakespeare's Dramatic Characters of Macbeth, Hamlet, Jacques, and Imogen. To Which are Prefixed and Introd.*

Snider, Denton. *Shakespeare's Tragedies.* New York: Cornell University Library, 2009.

5.12 Recommended Reading

Armstrong, Philip. *Shakespeare in Psychoanalysis.* London: Routledge, 2001.

Crystal, David and Crystal, Ben. *Shakespeare's Words: A Glossary and Language Companion.* London: Penguin Books, 2004.

Elliot, George. *Dramatic Providence in "Macbeth": A Study of Shakespeare's Tragic Theme of Humanity and Grace. With a Supplementary Essay on King Lear.* Connecticut Press, 1970.

Mousley, Andy. *Re-Humanising Shakespeare: Literary Humanism, Wisdom and Modernity.* Edinburgh: Edinburgh University Press, 2007.

Thornton, Mark and Ramona Wray. (Eds.) *Screening Shakespeare in the Twenty-First Century.* Edinburgh: Edinburgh University Press, 2006.

6
Structure

6.0 Objectives

After studying this unit, you will be able to understand the structure of the play, that is, the way various elements are organized to understand how a play could be analyzed to arrive at its meaning.

6.1 Introduction

Structure means the way in which the plot or the basic story is organized. The play, *Macbeth* has an excellent structure. It is considered as one of the best Shakespearean plays regarding structural aspects. Shakespeare has not introduced sub-plot or sub-plots to complicate the structure of the play. Every incident or speech is directly attached to the central character, the hero. The play is organized into five Acts. Each act contains several scenes. The plot is chronological.

6.2 Construction of the Plot

William Shakespeare has used language, structure and form very carefully to create anxiety and quickness in the play, *Macbeth*. The structure of a text means the way in which the events are arranged in the play. In *Macbeth*, the plot structure is chronological. The events in the play are presented to the audience in the order in which they happen. We discover that some events are described rather than shown on the stage, for instance, the action of Macbeth becoming the king. Some events happen offstage that is outside the sight of the audience, for example, Duncan's murder. Tragedies represent conflicts which end in catastrophe.

The events of the play, *Macbeth,* have been organized into five acts. Each act contains a number of scenes. Gustav Freytag, a German author in the nineteenth century designed a five act structure. He studied classical drama. He observed five stages in the organization of a tragic play. Exposition, rising action, climax, falling action and catastrophe are important stages in the structure of a play.

William Shakespeare has used poetic language in the writing of the play. For some part of the play he used language of the prose. The simple plot is always effective. *Macbeth* has one plot. It comprises one comic scene—the porter at the gate. This scene provides a relief to the horror of the assassination.

The introduction or exposition explains the situation. In Act I, early two scenes explain the situation of the play. The first scene brings us into the mystical atmosphere which pervades the entire play. The second scene describes the brave deeds of Macbeth. The rising action of the play begins in Act I, Scene III and continues to the Act III, Scene III. Macbeth returns from his victories. He is tempted to get the political power of the country. The three witches and Lady Macbeth prompt him for accomplishment of his aim. At length, he succeeds to achieve his main purpose.

The climax is the turning point in the play. In the climax, the reaction sets in against the hero. The climax occurs in the Act III, Scene III of the play, where Fleance escapes. Thus, Macbeth has not fully achieved what he strived for. He gets distracted by fears and hallucinations. He loses his self control in Act III, Scene IV. We know that he is doomed. The falling action runs with no obstacle from the banquet to the end of the play. Characters who were in the backdrop in the first scenes, now come to the frontage. Malcolm and Macduff personify the justice.

The catastrophe is the tragic end of the play. Macbeth has a double catastrophe. Lady Macbeth dies and Macbeth falls in the last act. Lady Macbeth walks in her sleep; and dies. Macbeth has done wrong to Macduff. Macduff kills Macbeth. Malcolm becomes the King of Scotland.

6.3 Elements of William Shakespeare's Tragedies

William Shakespeare is one of the most famous authors in English literature. He is well-known for writing tragedies. Tragedies written by him are widely studied and performed. We observe some important elements in Shakespearean tragedies:

- **Fatal Flaw:** A tragic flaw is a personality trait that leads to the downfall of the protagonist. He performs wrong action which brings his ruin. It is the most important element in a tragedy. All of the heroes/heroines in Shakespeare's tragedies have a weakness in personality. Their weakness leads them to their downfall. Macbeth's obsession with power, Othello's jealousy, and Hamlet's indecisiveness are the examples of tragic flaws in the tragic heroes.
- **Use of Supernatural Elements:** Use of supernatural elements is a common characteristic in the Elizabethan tragedies. Supernatural powers exert influence on the tragic hero's life.
- **Fall of the Nobleman:** The heroes in Shakespeare's tragedies are men in great position. They possess extreme wealth and power. It makes their downfall more tragic. Their fall affects the entire nation.
- **External Pressure:** Shakespeare's tragic heroes often fall victim to external pressure. Some evil spirits or manipulative characters exert pressure and bring their downfall.
- **Sympathy for Hero:** The audience develops sympathy for the hero. The hero possesses extraordinary knowledge and power but the tragic flaw brings his ruin.
- **The Protagonist's Good Character:** The protagonist in the Shakespearean tragedy is a man of character. He is destroyed by his own ego or desire for self-advancement. Ego overcomes his positive traits.

The Five Act Structure: Firm Organisation: William Shakespeare has taken his material from Holinshed's *Chronicles*. He skillfully reorganized it and made it a tremendously successful play. The characters are differentiated. Duncan is presented as a good and kind king. Macbeth is made into a brutal king. Banquo, the ancestor of King James, becomes an honest man. In Holinshed's *Chronicles*, he helps Macbeth to assassinate Duncan. The dramatist has given eminence to witches.

Act I: Exposition

The play opens with the introduction of three witches on the open place. They discuss about their plan to meet Macbeth on one heath, when the battle is over. The atmosphere is full of fear and terror. Macbeth has been already harbouring an ambition to be the monarch of Scotland. The witches stimulate his ambition by prophesying that he will be the King of Scotland. The beading sergeant gives a heroic account of Macbeth's bravery on the battlefield. Duncan praises him "O! Valiant cousin! worthy gentleman!"

When Macbeth has come to know the prophecy from the witches about his future, he starts thinking of assassination of Duncan to get the throne. But his conscience resists the evil thought. Macbeth is a complex character. The conflict between his ambition and conscience covers large part of his life. Lady Macbeth is more ambitious than her husband. Lady Macbeth is a woman of strong will power and ruthlessness. Because of his conscience, Macbeth is reluctant to commit the murder but he yields to her reasoning and force. Macbeth lacks the will. Had he possessed strong will power, he would have resisted his wife's instigation. We experience the feeling of terror and fear in Act I, it deals with the violence.

Act II: Complication

Macbeth and Lady Macbeth are moved by the passion of ambition. They hatch a conspiracy to murder King Duncan. Macbeth commits the murder. Before committing the murder, Macbeth sees a hallucination of a dagger. His conscience rebukes him that he should not do the evil action. After committing the murder, while coming back from Duncan's chamber, he listens to two people praying to God, but he cannot say the word, 'Amen.' A mysterious voice tells him that he has murdered the sleep. He feels a tremendous sense of guilt after committing the murder. Therefore, it is impossible for him to go back and smear the attendants with Duncan's blood and keep the daggers there. Lady Macbeth goes and smears the guards with blood so that they should be held guilty. She is confident. She thinks that a little water will clear them of the deed. Macbeth in a soliloquy says that whether all the oceans of the world can wash away stains of blood from his hand. Malcolm and Donalbain realize danger to their lives, they flee from Scotland.

Act III: Crisis

Banquo is killed by the murderers sent by Macbeth. Macbeth has thought that throne will go to Banquo's descendents. He also has thought that Banquo is morally superior to him; therefore his conscience is rebuked in his presence. Macbeth does not feel secure as long as Banquo is alive. Macbeth's plot against Banquo shows that he has already become a seasoned conspirator and criminal. Again because of his sense of guilt, Macbeth feels that Banquo's ghost is sitting in his chair at the time of state banquet. It is nothing but outward manifestation of the sense of the guilt. Lady Macbeth shows a rare presence of mind and saves the situation by sending away the guests. The meeting of the witches shows that their chief is also involved in their efforts to bring about the downfall of Macbeth. The murder of Banquo marks the climax of the rising action in the play. It also marks the beginning of the falling action.

Act IV: Resolution

Macbeth has now become very wicked. With his own initiative, he goes to meet the witches. The witches tell him to beware of Macduff; he can never be harmed by anyone born of a woman and he will never be defeated until the Birnam Wood moves to Dunsinane to fight against him. He feels very proud and secure. He comes to know that Macduff has fled to England. He slaughters Macduff's wife and children. Malcolm proposes to invade Scotland with the help of the English army, marks the beginning of the end for Macbeth.

Act V: Denouement: Retribution

Lady Macbeth dies and Macbeth is executed. Malcolm becomes a king. The denouement contains the catastrophe and the emotional climax. Lady Macbeth is afflicted by her conscience. She suffers from somnambulism. She is reminded of all the crimes committed. She dies. Macbeth too is now fed up with life. He compares himself to a yellow leaf of autumn. He becomes devoid of all emotions. He remains indifferent even to the news of his wife's death. On this occasion, he comments on the futility of human life. Macbeth also now realises the equivocation of the fiends. He calls the witches 'juggling fiends.' Retribution overtakes him. The agent of retribution is Macduff, whose family he has slaughtered. There is a moral order in this universe.

6.4 Three Unities

The action of Macbeth is well compact. William Shakespeare is little observant of the classical unities of time and place, but the unity of action is ever present in his dramas. The unity of action does not mean anything rigid as classical authorities suggested. For Shakespeare unity of action does not consist in concentrating interests on a single theme. In *Macbeth*, unity of action is strictly followed. William Shakespeare is the father of romantic drama; he has nothing to do with the classical unities of time, place, and action. Ben Jonson has been a champion of the classical unities. In the play, *Tempest*, Shakespeare has observed all unities but not too obviously like play of Jonson. *Macbeth* does not strictly observe the classical unities of time and place. It comes very close to the model of a play constructed on classical principles. The action of the play is compact and close-knit.

Macbeth has the quality of the unity of action. The unity of action creates a single impression. All the interest centers round the rise and fall of Macbeth. Every incident and every scene is related to fate of Macbeth. Few episodes have admitted into the play for giving comic relief, contrast, for giving the information regarding state of affairs in Scotland to the public.

Macbeth gets continuous success up to a certain point. There soon comes the ebb tide in his fortunes. The escape of Fleance is the first turning point in the play. In the first act, Macbeth meets the witches, they predict his future, and he follows the path of crime. In the second act, he commits the murder and gets the kingship at which he aimed. In the third act, his second crime is partly a success and partly a failure. Banquo is murdered and Fleance escapes. In the fourth act, he meets the witches again; formerly they supplied initiative to crime, now they breed in him the overconfidence—the sense of security which is mortal's chiefest enemy. Now his plans fail. Macduff has fled to Scotland. He commits the ridiculous crime of killing Macduff's wife and children. Thanes, nobles react against him, and bring his doom nearer. In the fifth act, retribution comes upon him. This is the main outline of the rise and fall of Macbeth. We observe that there is the organic unity in the development of the action.

The leading idea of the play is that crime brings its own punishment. In the beginning of his career Macbeth gets victory over Macdonwald and Sweno. His ambition is stimulated by success. Ambition is again encouraged by the witches' prophecy about his glorious future. To ensure the fulfillment of ambition, one crime leads to another. People of Scotland react against him. He becomes a victim of unceasing fear. His retribution begins with this fear and suspense. Macduff kills Macbeth in the battle. Lady Macbeth seems to possess strong will power, but it goes away under the assault of fear and suspense. Lady Macbeth broken in body and mind takes her own life. In both cases, it is true that evil brings its punishment. It is true that evil is self-destructive.

The whole of the play from beginning to the end is full of horror and terror. Darkness physical, mental and spiritual seems to have enveloped Scotland. Supernatural elements influence human fortunes. The witches appear in the very first scene in the atmosphere of thunder and lightning. Cruel murder is committed in the darkness of the night when owls shriek and nature begins to revolt. Murderer sees the blood stained dagger before his eyes. People cry aloud in the sleep. The porter at the gate of Macbeth's castle thinks that he is the gatekeeper of hell. Macbeth is a study in fear. It narrates the story that crime does not pay. Crime brings downfall.

6.5 Symbolism

(a) **The Baby Image and Its Symbolic Significance:** The baby-image appears continually in the play, *Macbeth*. Macbeth used it while showing pity for his victim-to-be, Duncan. Macbeth says:

A naked newborn babe,
Striding the blast, or heaven's cherubim, hors'd
Upon the sightless couriers of the air

The new-born babe is helpless. It is used as symbol for pity. The naked babe symbolizes helplessness and innocence. But it is also all powerful because it also symbolizes the future. Macbeth wages a war against future, and is destroyed as a consequence. The future is all powerful. Macbeth is defeated in his war against the future. Babe is the most powerful symbol in the tragedy.

Macbeth does not aspire for kingship for himself alone but is keen to establish a dynasty of kings. He kills Banquo for this reason only. Fleance escapes and Macbeth's plans are frustrated by the babe in person of him. Cleanth Brooks rightly said that there are a great many references to the babes in the play. The witches' prophecy has made a powerful impact on Macbeth. Macbeth hurriedly undertakes bloody action until he is totally ruined. Macbeth commits a series of murders. Because of his crimes, nobles are alienated. Macbeth is a great tragic protagonist like other tragic heroes, not because of his warrior courage and imagination but because of his attempt to conquer the future. Macbeth's war with the future ruins and destroys him.

Macbeth goes to the Weird sisters to know the future. Cleanth Brook says, "It is because of his hope for his own children and his fears of Banquo's that he visits the witches for counsel. It is altogether, appropriate, therefore, that two of the apparitions by which their counsel is revealed should be babe, the crowned babe and the bloody babe, for the babe signifies the future which Macbeth would control but cannot control. Earlier in the play, Macbeth, had declared that if the 'deed could trammel up the consequence,' he would be willing to jump the life to come. But he cannot jump the life to come. In his own terms he is betrayed, for it is idle to speak of jumping the life to come, if one yearns to found a line of kings. It is the babe that betrays Macbeth—his own babes, most of all. Macbeth's distraught mind, thus, forces him to make war on children, a war which in itself reflects his desperation and is confession of weakness."

The babe is a rich complex symbol which symbolizes pity, innocence, and future. It also symbolizes emotional ties which make man more than machine. Child is the symbol of the future. Macbeth has put trust in prophecies. The last prophecy concerns the child. Macduff declare to Macbeth that he was not 'born of woman' but was from his 'Mother's womb untimely ripped.' The naked babe also symbolizes essential humanity. In the robes of honour one should never forget essential humanity, otherwise one will be ruined.

(b) **Cloak and Mask Imagery:** One of the recurrent symbols is that of a robe too big for the wearer so that the dress has a humiliating and degrading impact. New honour sits ill upon Macbeth and the idea is recurrently conveyed by comparing these honours to a loose and badly fitting garment belonging to someone else. Ross greets him as Thane of Cawdor. Macbeth quickly replies:

> The thane of Cawdor lives. Why do you dress me
> In borrowed robes

When Lady Macbeth urges her husband to murder Duncan, he is reluctant to do the deed. He gives three reasons for not going ahead with it. He tells that he has lately been honoured by the king, people think well of him, he should reap the reward of these things and not upset everything by this murder which they have planned. He uses the metaphor of clothes:

> I have bought
> Golden opinions from all sorts of people,
> Which would be worn now in their newest gloss?
> Not cast aside so soon.

Angus vividly tells the essence of what people have been thinking about Macbeth's accession to power:

> Now does he feel his title
> Hang loose about him, like a giant's robe
> Upon a dwarfish thief

6.6 Soliloquies and Asides

William Shakespeare has used soliloquies and asides comprehensively in this play as in other foremost tragedies.

These asides and soliloquies are important from the point of view of plot development and character revelation. Asides and soliloquies comprise philosophy and profound thinking about human life. They are indispensable to the play for philosophical and psychological interest. There is the distinction between aside and soliloquy. Aside is a speech given by an actor that is intended to be heard by the audience but not by the other characters on stage. Soliloquy is speaking one's thoughts aloud, especially when a character does this without another character being present on stage.

Macbeth and Banquo while returning victorious from the battlefield, are greeted by Ross and Angus. They inform him that King has conferred the title of Thane of Cawdor upon him. In an aside, he says to himself: "Glamis, and Thane of Cawdor, the greatest is behind." Only a moment later in the second aside he says to himself that the prophecies made by the witches cannot be evil and that they cannot be beneficial either. If these prophecies were evil, he would not have been honoured with the title Thane of Cawdor. If they were beneficial, there would not have arisen in his mind a horrible thought. The horrible thought which has arisen in his mind is the assassination of King Duncan to get the throne for himself. In the other aside, he says that if chance will have him as the king, chance should be allowed to operate without there being any need for him to make an effort. Then he says that time and tide wait for no man and that what is to happen must happen. These asides are very important dramatically because they mark the birth of evil in Macbeth's mind. These asides give us information about the character of Macbeth.

When King Duncan announces Malcolm as the heir to the throne, Macbeth in the aside says that nomination of Malcolm has become a hurdle in the way of the achievement of his ambition. Then he realizes the nature of the crime that he must commit, he calls upon the stars to extinguish their light so that his black and deep desires are not known to himself. He has become conscious of the wickedness of the desire. He cannot suppress the wicked desire which has arisen in his mind. He is not ready to listen to the voice of conscience which tells him that the path which he has chosen will lead him to damnation.

Macbeth's soliloquy in Act I, Scene VII gives us information about what he thinks about his conspiracy of assassination of King Duncan. He thinks of the evil consequences of the horrible deed. He knows that justice compels a man to drink the very cup of poison which he has prepared for someone else. Duncan is his sovereign, kinsman, and the benefactor whom he should protect from other murderers rather than himself becoming a murderer. He has been a gentle and kind hearted king; murder of Duncan would arouse not only anger and resentment of the people, but their deep sympathies. He says that because of his inordinate ambition only he is thinking of the murder of Duncan. This soliloquy reveals us the state of mind of Macbeth. He is a man of intellect and imagination. He has the capacity to probe his own motives.

Macbeth makes his soliloquy when he is ready to Murder Duncan, and he is preparing to go into Duncan's bedroom where Duncan is asleep. Macbeth sees a hallucination of a dagger. Macbeth finds drops of blood on its blade and on its handle. This soliloquy shows the sense of guilt operating upon Macbeth. He is completely conscious of the wickedness of the deed. It depicts Macbeth's mind at the crucial moment.

After committing the murder Macbeth's mind is completely overwhelmed by the sense of guilt. Looking at his hands he feels that all the water of Great Ocean cannot wash the blood from them. On the contrary, he feels that green water will turn into red.

When Macbeth has ruled as a king for some time, he feels that Banquo poses a threat to him. He says that Banquo is a man of genuine qualities; in Banquo's presence his conscience feels uneasy. He was also uneasy because of the witches' prediction that the throne would pass to Banquo's descendents. He thinks that throne should pass to his children only.

When Macbeth gets the news of the English forces approaching Dunsinane, he speaks about the futility of human life. He says that the present crisis in his life will either strengthen his position forever or will unthrone him. He feels that he has lived long enough and that his present condition may be compared to a leaf which has turned yellow with the coming of autumn. He has become hardened by committing crimes.

In the soliloquy in the ending of the play, Macbeth expresses confidence that he will not be killed by a man born of a woman. He realizes the peril. He compares his position to a bear which has been tied to a stake to be attacked by hounds. He tells that he will not kill himself; rather he will fight in the battle. Macduff kills him in the battle.

After reading a letter from her husband, Lady Macbeth expresses her thoughts in the soliloquy. She says that by witches' prophecy her husband will soon become the king. At the same time, she knows that her husband "is too full of the milk of human kindness." She says her husband is ambitious but he does not possess wickedness which should accompany ambition.

In the soliloquy in Act III, Scene II, Lady Macbeth tells that things are not running smoothly. She says Duncan is enjoying peace in his grave. Her feeling is shared by Macbeth who says that existence of Banquo has become a thorn for them. These soliloquies express Macbeth and Lady Macbeth's states of minds.

6.7 Check your Progress

(1) Write a note on the plot construction of the play, *Macbeth*.

(2) What are the prominent elements of William Shakespeare's tragedies?

(3) Explain the rule of Three Unities with reference to Macbeth.

(4) What important symbols has Shakespeare used in *Macbeth?*

(5) What is the value and significance of soliloquy in *Macbeth?*

6.8 Key to Check your Progress

(1) For answer see 6.2

(2) For answer see 6.3

(3) For answer see 6.4

(4) For answer see 6.5

(5) For answer see 6.6

6.9 Summary

In this unit, we have learnt the elements which form a play. Plot construction is an important technique. The success of the play depends on the proper organization of various elements in the structure of the play. We have also seen that dramatist uses symbols to reveal the mystery of human life. Soliloquies and asides are used to explicate the state of the mind of the characters. The study of structural aspects of the play is important to understand the drama properly.

6.10 Glossary

- Sergeant—a non-commissioned army officer with a rank above a corporal
- Conscience—a person's awareness of right or wrong with regard to her or his own thoughts and actions
- Ruthlessness—having or showing no pity or feeling foe others; hard and cruel
- Daggers—a short pointed knife used as a weapon
- Banquet—a large formal meal usually for a special event at which speeches are often made
- Resolution—the action of solving or settling problems, doubts, etc.
- Denouement—the last part, made especially of a book, play, etc. in which everything is clear
- Retribution—punishment that is considered to be morally right and fully deserved
- Symbolism—the use of symbols to represent things, especially in art and literature.

6.11 Further Reading

Adelman, Janet. "Born of Woman: Fantasies of Maternal Power in *Macbeth*." *Cannibals, Witches, and Divorce: Estranging the Renaissance*. Ed. Marjorie Garber. Baltimore: Johns Hopkins University Press, 1987. 90-121.

Berger, Harry Jr. "The Early Scenes of *Macbeth:* Preface to a New Interpretation." *ELH* 47 (1980): 1-31.

Brooks, Cleanth. "The Naked Babe and the Cloak of Manliness." *The Well Wrought Urn: Studies in the Structure of Poetry.* 1947. San Diego: Harcourt, 1974. 22-49.

Foakes, R.A. "Images of Death: Ambition in *Macbeth.*" *Focus on Macbeth*. Ed. John Russell Brown. London: Routledge, 1982. 7-29.

6.12 Recommended Reading

Aristotle. *The Nicomachean Ethics*. Trans. Harris Rackham. Hertfordshire: Wordsworth Editions, 1996.

Felperin, Howard. *Shakespearean Representation: Mimesis and Modernity in Elizabethan Tragedy.* Princeton: Princeton University Press, 1977.

Frye, Northrop. *Fools of Time: Studies in Shakespearean Tragedy.* Toronto: University of Toronto Press, 1967.

Scragg, Leah. *Discovering Shakespeare's Meaning: An Introduction to the Study of Shakespeare's Dramatic Structure.* London: Longman.

Wilson, Harold S. *On the Design of Shakespearean Tragedy.* Toronto: University of Toronto Press, 1957.

7
Conclusion

In this unit, we have studied the major critics who have provided valuable insights into *Macbeth*. The observations made by the critics help us to understand various thematic and structural aspects of the play. The problem of tragedy has always been the problem of evil in the world. The tragedy explicates the important concerns, the evil that befalls men and reasons for the evil. Therefore, tragedy shares many things with philosophy and spiritualism.

William Shakespeare is the greatest dramatist of all time. He has written thirty-seven plays, one hundred fifty-four sonnets, and five long narrative poems. All are classics. His dramas are an exploration of the influence of passions in human life. Every human being translates his thoughts into action. Virtuous thoughts bring one glory, peace and happiness whereas vicious thoughts lead one to evil actions which bring sorrow, suffering and death. God rewards virtuous people, He punishes evil people. He inflicts punishment upon men for their cruel actions.

William Shakespeare above all concerns with the passions and their role in human life. Passion means an intense desire to possess estate, honour and great places. His plays offer moral philosophy which is relevant for all ages. It is the truth well accepted that virtuous actions bring happiness. Tragedies give the warning that false courage, temptations; greed might lead a person to wrong action, which might be responsible for destruction of the person who performs evil deed.

To comprehend human life has always been a question which has been being debated in all ages. Human life is mysterious and full of opportunities, temptations and difficulties. Prosperity can never be taken into granted. It is uncertain. The people in great positions, prosperity fall; the reason are vices or wrong passions. Virtues help people to avoid misery and get happiness. History is full of evidence that evil persons are punished, virtuous people are rewarded. Tragedies offer people the lessons of moral philosophy.

Macbeth deals with themes of ambition and fear. Ambition has been the overriding passion in the play. Macbeth is the military general and trusted kinsman of the king, and then also he assassinates King Duncan of Scotland to get kingship for himself. He becomes a criminal. He does the crime as per his free will. Moral values do not stop him from committing the heinous crime, because he does not listen to the voice of conscience within him. The passion of ambition has been so overriding that the voice of conscience proved feeble.

According to Dr. Samuel Johnson, a famous critic, while doing true estimate of abilities and merits of a writer, it is always necessary to examine the true genius of the age and the opinions of his contemporaries. William Shakespeare introduces three witches, supernatural elements in the play. In contemporary time, these things are treated as improbable. In William Shakespeare's time people believed in the supernatural elements and witches. There prevailed the darkness of ignorance and credulity in the period, people believed in their presence. In all ages, common people and even some learned people believed in the enchantment and witchcraft.

King Duncan is intelligent, generous, trusting and a good ruler of Scotland. He cannot read the mind of the people. He admits that there is no art to know the dark desires in the minds of the trusted people. He could not identify Thane of Cawdor's treachery in advance. His spies also could not inform him. He is the representative of a good king. King Duncan is soft and generous. He is killed because of his softness, childish trust, and the inability to read mind's of his officers.

King Duncan bestows the title of the Prince of Cumberland upon Malcolm. Macbeth becomes aware of his dark desires, when king announces the heir to the throne. He appeals the stars to conceal the light, so that his dark desires will be unknown to the people. He becomes infatuated by the lust for power. He becomes slave to the passion of ambition. He gives in to the evil desires expressed by his wife, Lady Macbeth. He assassinates King Duncan in his sleep, and grabs the throne for himself. After becoming the King of Scotland, he does not stop crime. He has become a criminal king. To make his position secure, he kills Banquo by hiring murderers, attempts to kill Fleance, but he manages to escape. Macbeth kills Macduff's family, many other minions whom he considers dangerous for his position. Macbeth kills young Siward. In the end of the play, Macduff kills Macbeth and the tyrant's rule has come to an end. Malcolm becomes the King of Scotland. He represented all the virtues of a great and ideal ruler. He is crowned at Scone. He is intelligent, cares for the protection and welfare of the people.

The character of Malcolm is based on the King Malcolm III of Scotland, derived largely from the account of *Holinshed's Chronicles of England, Scotland, and Ireland*. Malcolm represents all the virtues which a king is expected to possess.

Macbeth believes in the prophecy made by three witches. They predicted that he will become the King of Scotland. They have not told him how he will achieve monarchy. The three witches represent Macbeth's evil emotions and thoughts. When King Duncan announces Malcolm as the heir to throne, Macbeth becomes restless because he considers the declaration as an obstacle for his ambition to be the King. He appeals the stars in the sky that his deep dark desires may not be visible to the people in the court. Because of his dark evil desires he chooses the wrong path to become the king. He is a psychopath. He is ready to do anything to get the position of king for himself. He does not listen to the voice of conscience within him which advises him not to proceed in the evil business.

Macbeth killed many people to consolidate his position of kingship. He brutally murders Macduff's family. When Macduff learns of the massacre of his family, he vows to avenge the brutal massacre of his family. With the help of the English army, Malcolm along with Siward, with other nobles wages a war against Macbeth to dethrone him.

The three witches have told Macbeth that his life is protected by a charm, therefore, he believes that he will not be killed by a man born of woman and he will not be defeated till the Birnam Wood moves to Dunsinane. He thought that a forest never moves from its place, therefore, he is invincible. Macbeth is in illusion that the charm will protect his life from all kinds of difficulties and dangers. Macduff tells him that he is the person who is born in the caesarean method. The soldiers in the force covered themselves behind the branches of trees of Birnam Wood. When the force is moving towards Dunsinane, the spectacle is such that as if Birnam Wood is moving to Dunsinane. In the battle, Macduff cuts off the head of the tyrant. Macbeth has been killed by Macduff. Malcolm becomes the King of Scotland.

Literature is the mirror to society. The study of literature gives us important and valuable lessons of human life. The play provides an insight into human life. Virtues bring success, prosperity, wealth in human life whereas vices bring death, destruction, chaos, sorrow and suffering. Ambition, greed and fear mislead Macbeth. He commits horrible crimes of killing his nobles; he fears that they are danger to his position. To make his throne secure, he commits heinous crimes; thereby he brings his own life in trouble.

The study of the play makes us familiar about the reasons of the downfall of the great men from prosperity to adversity, from life to death. The tragedy warns people of evil action which bring destruction and chaos. God punishes evil rulers in all nations. Vices are responsible for the fall of tragic hero. Macbeth has over ambition, which prompts him for the assassination of King Duncan. Human beings must have control of conscience over their passions; otherwise passions bring sorrow, suffering and death. *Macbeth* explores the passions of ambition fear. Ambition and fear move Macbeth and Lady Macbeth to rash deeds.

The famous critic, Lily Campbell has said that Macbeth is a play which analyses the theme of fear and its impact on human life. The passions of ambition, lust, and greed compel men to commit sinful actions which bring sorrow and death. According to Professor Bradley, the tragic suffering occurs because of collision not with the fate but with the moral power in the world.

Dr. Samuel Johnson is of the view that we should distinguish between true and false courage. William Shakespeare has possessed a great knowledge of human nature. Lady Macbeth argues with Macbeth to commit the murder, she reminds Macbeth of the excellence and dignity of courage. According to Aristotle, true courage is doing the right action even in the fearful atmosphere.

According to great critic, Samuel Coleridge, there is the relationship between cause and effect. Had Macbeth possessed strong moral will, he would not have committed heinous crimes. Macbeth should not have been the victim of temptation of power, but he should have been the master of emotions and passions. We transform our thoughts into action. Banquo is true to nature. Witches could tempt Macbeth but they could not lure Banquo because he is in true possession of himself.

William Shakespeare is the greatest dramatist of all time. Drama is the mirror of human life. We understand the important aspects and facets of human life through the study of plays. Drama offers us wisdom and values which help us to elevate the dignity of our lives. It gives comprehensive knowledge of human life. *Macbeth* is a great play which gives us a rich philosophy life and it makes us aware about the effects of passions of ambition, fear, and courage on our actions.

7.1 Recommended Reading

Bradley, A.C. *Shakespearean Tragedy: Lectures on Hamlet, Othello, King Lear, Macbeth*. New York: Penguin, 1991.

Campbell, Lily Bess. *Shakespeare's Tragic Heroes: Slaves of Passion*. New York: Cambridge University Press, 2009.

Coleridge, Samuel Taylor; Foakes, R.A.; Collier, John. Eds. *Coleridge on Shakespeare: The Text of the Lectures of 1811-12*. London: Routledge, 2005.

Gaskin, Richard. *Language, Truth, and Literature: A Defence of Literary Humanism*. Oxford: Oxford University Press, 2016.

Johnson, Samuel. *Dr. Johnson on Shakespeare*. London: Penguin Books, 1997.